I0013348

The Role of Social Media in Society

Society

A Simple Guide to Big Ideas

Nova Martian

2

Contents

4

Chapter 1

Understanding Social Media

This chapter lays the conceptual foundation for our exploration of social media. We begin by defining social media and its ecosystem, then trace its historical evolution. Next, we categorize the major platform types, unpack the universal features that drive engagement, analyze why people use these networks, and conclude by examining access inequalities and strategies for inclusion.

1.1 Defining Social Media

The term "social media" might seem self-evident today, but its history and meaning remain surprisingly fluid. Coined in the late 1990s and gaining mass currency in the early 2000s, "social media" originally described web-based platforms that enabled user interaction, distinct from static webpages. Over time, its scope has broadened dramatically, encompassing a diverse ecosystem where people not only consume content but also create, share, and engage dynamically. Social media is no longer just a technological innovation; it has become a cultural and communicative revolution shaping how information circulates, identities form, and communities emerge.

At its core, social media is defined by a few essential characteristics that distinguish it from prior forms of media and communication. First, the content it features is overwhelmingly *user-generated*. Unlike traditional media outlets—newspapers, television, or radio—where experts or journalists craft and distribute content to passive audiences, social media platforms empower users themselves to produce and publish text, images, videos, and more. This democratization of content creation has lowered barriers to participation, enabling voices from all corners to be heard.

Second, *interactivity* forms a fundamental pillar. People do not merely consume content; they actively respond to it through likes, comments, shares, and other feedback mechanisms. This two-way flow fosters rich conversations and collaborations, transforming media from a monologue into a dialogue. Lastly, social media inherently relies on *networked communication*. Users are linked not only to the platform but also to each other, creating webs of connections where information travels horizontally and diagonally, rather than just flowing down a hierarchical or linear channel.

This many-to-many communication model sets social media apart. Traditional media typically operates on a one-to-many basis: a broadcaster or publisher sends the same message to a large, often anonymous audience. Social media breaks from this model by enabling multidirectional exchanges. For example, a single post on Twitter or Facebook may spark entire conversations, with multiple users replying, retweeting, or remixing the content in unpredictable ways. This amplifies the dynamism and complexity of information flows, allowing social trends to emerge virally and communities to self-organize around shared interests or causes.

Integral to these processes are the profiles that users create and curate on these platforms. Unlike a mere username on a bulletin board, social media profiles often function as digital identities—carefully constructed presentations of the self. Users choose how to represent themselves through photos, bios, posted content, and interactions with others. This performative aspect encourages both authenticity and creativity but also invites questions about privacy, authenticity, and the boundaries between public and private spheres. For many, profiles serve as personal branding tools, enabling them to signal affiliation, expertise, or personality traits to a broad audience.

Underlying these profiles is the *networked structure* of relationships—often described through the notion of a *social graph*. Platforms map connections between users, whether through "friendships," "followers," or other linkage models. These relationships dictate the flow of information and influence, as well as the scope of visibility for any given post or interaction. The shape of one's network can deeply affect one's social experience: tightly knit clusters foster strong ties and intimate exchanges, while broader networks enable the circulation of ideas across diverse groups and communities.

Communities flourish within social media not only by virtue of these networks but also through explicit collectivities such as groups, pages, and hashtags. Groups offer dedicated spaces for members to discuss specific topics, organize events, or mobilize action, often moderated to maintain focus and civility. Pages function as hubs for organizations, celebrities, or interest groups to engage followers. Meanwhile, hashtags provide a grassroots, user-driven way to aggregate content around themes, events, or campaigns, transcending formal group boundaries and connecting users across the platform. Together, these tools scaffold a mosaic of collective identity and participation.

The interactive nature of social media is further reinforced by continuous feedback loops. Users react in real time through likes, emoji reactions, comments, and shares, enabling instant social validation or critique. This immediacy creates a sense of presence and urgency, fostering engagement but also sometimes amplifying polarization or misinformation. Platforms constantly refine these interactive mechanisms, incorporating algorithmic feeds that prioritize popular or relevant content, further shaping how users experience and contribute to the social media landscape.

Behind this vibrant ecosystem lies a complex web of stakeholders with distinct and often competing interests. The primary actors, *users*, are both content creators and consumers—they generate data that fuels the platform's activity while seeking connection, entertainment, or information. *Platform providers* like Facebook, Twitter, or Instagram design and maintain the technological infrastructure, establishing rules and features to optimize engagement and growth. Advertisers and marketers constitute another crucial group, leveraging the platforms' targeting capabilities to reach audiences with personalized messages, thus monetizing user attention. Finally, *regulators* and policymakers weigh in to address concerns around privacy, misinformation, and market dominance, shaping the evolving governance of social media spaces.

Bringing these threads together, social media can be defined as: *a collection of internet-based platforms and tools that enable users to create, share, and interact with content in a networked environment characterized by many-to-many communication, facilitated by profiles and social connections,*

4

and supported by an ecosystem of users, platform providers, advertisers, and regulators. This definition captures not only the technological dimensions but also the social and economic dynamics that make social media a defining feature of contemporary life.

Understanding social media through this multifaceted lens reveals why it matters far beyond mere technology. It is a dynamic social system in which identities are constructed, communities formed, conversations sparked, and influence negotiated—a space where private voices become public actors and where information flows reshape politics, culture, and everyday social interaction. Defining it carefully lays the groundwork to explore its promises and pitfalls in the chapters ahead.

1.2 A Brief History of Social Media

Social media as we know it today did not appear overnight; it is the culmination of several distinct phases, each building upon prior technological innovations and shifting user behaviors. To truly appreciate the landscape of contemporary social platforms, we must first understand their roots in early online communities, which laid the groundwork for the interactive, interconnected digital experiences we now take for granted.

Before the Web became a ubiquitous portal for social interaction, enthusiasts connected through bulletin board systems (BBS), Usenet newsgroups, and Internet Relay Chat (IRC) chatrooms in the 1980s and early 1990s. BBS allowed users to dial into servers via modems to post messages, share files, and engage in discussions—a remarkably intimate and local experience by today's standards. Meanwhile, Usenet functioned as a distributed collection of discussion forums organized into topics called newsgroups, enabling conversations to persist asynchronously across the globe. IRC brought real-time chatrooms, where users could join channels to exchange instant messages or private texts, pioneering a more spontaneous and conversational form of online socializing. These platforms fostered niche communities of shared interests but were limited by text-only interfaces and rudimentary connectivity.

The advent of the World Wide Web set the stage for the first social networking pioneers in the late 1990s and early 2000s. Among these, SixDegrees.com emerged in 1997 as one of the earliest platforms to allow users to create profiles and establish friend lists in a way that visually represented a social graph. Despite its innovative concept, SixDegrees struggled with limited network effects and technical constraints, ultimately shutting down in 2001. Friendster followed in 2002, offering enhanced profile customization, friend connections, and the notion of "friends of friends" to expand social reach. Friendster attracted millions but fell short in scaling infrastructure and maintaining user engagement during its rapid growth. Both platforms underscored a key realization: social networks depended not just on features but on vibrant, active communities and reliable performance.

The mid-2000s saw the rise of MySpace and Facebook, which would define many conventions of social media still visible today. MySpace, launched in 2003, democratized profile personalization, allowing users to embed music, images, and background themes. Its open platform appealed primarily to musicians and youth culture, fostering a visually expressive and creatively driven social experience. Meanwhile, Facebook (initially accessible only to college students) emphasized clean, standardized profiles, centralized news feeds, and clearly defined friend networks, promoting a more streamlined and intimate sense of connectivity. Importantly, Facebook's News Feed—introduced in 2006—revolutionized how content was consumed by aggregating updates from friends, creating a dynamic and constantly refreshed pulse of social life. Together, MySpace and Facebook standardized profiles, friend-centric networks, and activity streams, setting the template for many successors.

With the proliferation of broadband Internet and cheaper multimedia devices, media sharing platforms transformed social media from text and links to rich, user-generated audiovisual content. YouTube, launched in 2005, quickly became the dominant hub for sharing videos, from homemade clips to professionally produced content. It empowered users to not only consume but also broadcast to mass audiences, blurring the lines between creators and viewers. Flickr, also established in 2004, similarly revolutionized online photo sharing by combining high-quality storage with social features such as tagging and commenting, allowing photographic communities to emerge and flourish. These platforms highlighted how compelling visual media could deepen engagement and foster creative expression among users worldwide.

The emergence of microblogging further reshaped how people communicated online. Twitter, founded in 2006, popularized the concept of short-form, real-time updates limited initially to 140 characters, later doubled to 280. This novel brevity encouraged spontaneity, immediacy, and breadth over depth, enabling users to share thoughts, news, and reactions in rapid, digestible bursts. Twitter became especially valuable during breaking news events, social movements, and celebrity interactions, illustrating how concise, public discourse could influence broader cultural conversations. The microblogging format also catalyzed the rise of hashtags, memes, and viral chains, making individual voices part of a global conversation.

The next seismic shift in social media coincided with the ascendance of smartphones and mobile apps. The mobile-first paradigm redefined both access and design: users were no longer tethered to desktops but carried social platforms in their pockets, ready for instant engagement. Interfaces became sleeker, touch-optimized, and designed for quick interactions during everyday moments. App stores created convenient distribution channels, while push notifications demanded real-time attention. This mobile revolution fueled the rise of Instagram (2010) with its visual storytelling and ephemeral appeal, Snapchat (2011) with disappearing messages, and TikTok (2016) with short, algorithmically driven video streams. Mobile's ubiquity also intensified users' continuous engagement, embedding social media deeper into daily routines than ever before.

Concomitant with the mobile boom was the rise of private messaging and ephemeral content, adding layers of intimacy and immediacy to social interactions. WhatsApp, acquired by Facebook in 2014, capitalized on seamless, encrypted messaging among contacts worldwide, bypassing traditional SMS and enabling rich media sharing. Snapchat innovated with messages and stories that disappeared after being viewed, fostering candid self-expression without permanent digital footprints. These trends reflected evolving desires for privacy, authenticity, and transient communication, broadening social media beyond public broadcasting to include encrypted, fleeting exchanges within trusted circles.

Live streaming and interactive media have become increasingly prominent in the current social media ecosystem, offering real-time video broadcasts combined with direct audience participation. Platforms such as Twitch, and later, features integrated into Facebook, Instagram, and TikTok, empower creators to connect instantly with viewers through chats, polls, and reactions, creating vibrant digital performances and communities. Live streaming has democratized content creation further, enabling anyone with a smartphone and internet connection to become a broadcaster. This phenomenon also reflects a shift from passive consumption to engaged, participatory entertainment, influencing marketing, politics, education, and social activism alike.

Year	Platform or Milestone	Significance
1978	Bulletin Board Systems (BBS)	Early dial-up message boards for community exchange
1980s	Usenet Newsgroups	Distributed asynchronous topic-based discussions
1988	Internet Relay Chat (IRC)	Real-time group and private chatting
1997	SixDegrees.com	First social network with profiles and friend lists
2002	Friendster	Early broad social networking with friend-of-friend expansion
2003	MySpace	Popularized profile customization and youth culture networks
2004	Facebook	Standardized profiles, friend networks, and News Feed
2004	Flickr	Revolutionized photo sharing with social features
2005	YouTube	Transformed video sharing into mass user-generated content
2006	Twitter	Microblogging with short, real-time updates and hashtags
2010	Instagram	Mobile-first photo sharing with social discovery
2011	Snapchat	Ephemeral messaging and stories fostering candid communication
2016	TikTok	Algorithm-driven short video platform fueling viral creativity
2020s	Live Streaming	Enhanced audience interaction via real-time broadcasts

Table 1.1: Key Platforms and Milestones in Social Media History

The trajectory from early text-based communities to today's richly interactive, mobile-centric platforms reflects profound technological and social shifts. Initially, limited bandwidth and nascent interfaces restricted online socializing to text and modest file exchanges. As connectivity and multimedia tools advanced, social media embraced images, videos, and real-time communication, diversifying the modes and rhythms of online interaction. Meanwhile, evolving user expectations moved from public broadcasting towards private, ephemeral, and highly personalized experiences. The rise of smartphones did not simply add convenience; it transformed how, when, and why people engage socially online, embedding digital networks ever deeper in everyday life.

This history is not merely a chronology of platforms but a reflection of how technology and society continually reshape one another. Each innovation responded to unmet needs or frustrations with previous models—be it the desire for richer media, more spontaneity, greater privacy, or heightened interactivity. Understanding these phases helps us appreciate social media's complex role in contemporary culture, and prepares us to anticipate its next transformations, as new technologies and user behaviors emerge on the horizon.

1.3   Types of Social Media Platforms

Classifying social media platforms by their primary function offers clarity amid the sprawling digital landscape. While all such platforms facilitate connection and communication, their design, features, and typical usage diverge significantly. Understanding these distinctions helps users—from casual browsers to marketers—select tools attuned to their specific goals, whether that means building networks, sharing creative content, or engaging in focused discussions. This taxonomy can be thought of as a practical map, categorizing platforms according to how they enable interaction and what kind of content or community they prioritize.

Social Networking Sites

At the core of social media's early evolution lie social networking sites, the archetypal platforms designed to mirror real-world relationships in a digital sphere. Sites like Facebook and LinkedIn exemplify this category, each offering scaffolding for distinct kinds of connections. Facebook centers on personal relationships, encouraging users to share life updates, photos, and event invitations with friends and family. Its algorithm fosters a continuous, multidimensional social feed where private and public interactions intertwine.

In contrast, LinkedIn carves out a professional space, prioritizing career-oriented connections, endorsements, and job-seeking opportunities. Here, the content shared tends toward expertise, industry news, and professional achievements, reflecting a more curated and goal-driven network. Both platforms rely heavily on user profiles as identity anchors, but the social context—personal versus professional—shapes interaction patterns and content types.

Media Sharing Platforms

Visual storytelling reigns supreme on media sharing platforms, which prioritize images, videos, and increasingly short-form creative content. Instagram's original appeal lies in its clean, mobile-first interface for sharing photographs and short videos, catalyzing communities from fashion influencers to amateur photographers. Over time, it has morphed into a commercial and cultural hub, blending personal expression with brand marketing.

YouTube's strength rests on video content of any length and subject, nurturing everything from informal vlogs to elaborate educational series. It's a platform where creators can monetize content and cultivate dedicated audiences. TikTok, the newest major entrant, revolutionized media sharing by emphasizing algorithm-driven, bite-sized videos meant for rapid consumption and viral trends. The platform's playful, ephemeral style highlights creativity and immediacy, attracting a younger demographic and redefining video engagement norms.

These platforms excel when visual impact catalyzes attention and message retention, making them ideal for creators, entertainers, and marketers seeking immersive storytelling or viral reach.

Discussion Forums

For those craving depth, nuance, and community-driven knowledge exchange, discussion forums present a distinct social media category. Platforms like Reddit organize conversations around thematic "subreddits," enabling threaded discussions that persist indefinitely. This structure supports layered dialogues with nested replies, fostering detailed debates, troubleshooting, and shared interests.

Specialized forums—ranging from technology and gaming to parenting or niche hobbies—allow participants to self-select communities where expertise or enthusiasm thrive. Unlike the chronological feed of many platforms, forums prioritize topical relevance and community moderation, creating spaces where collective memory and norms evolve organically.

Their strengths lie in sustained engagement and the cultivation of insider knowledge, making them invaluable for crowdsourced problem-solving and peer support.

Microblogging Services

Microblogging services distill social expression into concise bursts, typically limited by character count but amplified by real-time distribution and broad followership. Twitter pioneered this format, offering a public arena for rapid news sharing, commentary, and conversational threads. Its simplicity—an emphasis on brevity and immediacy—has made it essential for journalists, thought leaders, and activists.

Mastodon and similar decentralized platforms replicate this microblogging style but with an emphasis on user autonomy, community governance, and reduced corporate oversight. These services highlight the social media principle that small textual glimpses can catalyze large-scale discourse, whether in trending hashtags or focused interest groups.

Microblogging's appeal lies in its agility as a tool for public updates, alerts, and social listening, suited to fast-paced information environments.

Messaging and Group Chat Apps

Behind the public faces of social media lie messaging and group chat applications, which emphasize private, synchronous, or semi-synchronous communication. Apps like WhatsApp and Telegram combine direct messaging, group chats, voice notes, and increasingly, multimedia sharing, supporting close-knit social circles or collaborative teams.

Discord, originally popular with gaming communities, extends this model into rich-server environments where users engage via text, voice, and video channels. Its layered permissions and customizable bots enable vibrant group dynamics often organized around shared passions or work projects.

While less about broad broadcasting, these apps excel at fostering intimacy and immediacy in communication, filling a niche for trusted interaction and community maintenance beyond public timelines.

Professional and Niche Networks

Beyond general social or media sharing platforms, specialized networks serve discrete professional or creative audiences. GitHub, for example, is a collaborative hub for software development, where version control meets social coding, and projects evolve in public repositories complemented by peer feedback.

ResearchGate focuses on scientists and academics, facilitating paper sharing, collaboration, and impact tracking within scholarly communities. Meanwhile, platforms like Behance cater to creatives, showcasing portfolios across design, photography, and illustration.

These niche networks combine domain-specific tools with social functions, cultivating environments where expertise and professional identity converge, supporting career development and specialized knowledge exchange.

Blogging and Publishing Platforms

Long-form content finds a home on blogging and publishing platforms, which blend personal expression with public dissemination. WordPress empowers users with customizable websites and blogs, ranging from personal diaries to full-scale editorial operations. Medium adopts a cleaner, more social approach, inviting writers to publish essays, reports, and stories that can be easily discovered and shared.

These platforms emphasize narrative depth and reflective content, often enabling monetization or audience building through subscriptions and curated highlights. Their value resides in providing space for sustained argumentation, storytelling, and thought leadership beyond the brevity of other social media formats.

Platform Taxonomy Summary

To synthesize, social media platforms can be functionally grouped as follows:

Category	Primary Function	Typical Uses
Social Networking Sites	Connecting people personally or professionally	Maintaining relationships, sharing updates
Media Sharing Platforms	Visual and audiovisual content distribution	Creative expression, marketing, entertainment
Discussion Forums	Thematic threaded conversations	Knowledge sharing, community building
Microblogging Services	Short public updates and conversations	News sharing, trend participation
Messaging and Group Chat Apps	Private or group communication	Intimate, real-time interaction
Professional and Niche Networks	Domain-specific collaboration	Career development, expert networking
Blogging and Publishing Platforms	Long-form content	Storytelling, analysis, thought leadership

Each category serves distinct communication goals, though real-world platforms often blend features, reflecting the fluidity of online social interaction.

Choosing Platforms by Purpose

Selecting the right platform depends on understanding both your communication objectives and the audience you wish to engage. For personal relationship maintenance or broad social integration, general social networking sites like Facebook are effective. If visual storytelling or brand promotion is the goal, platforms such as Instagram or TikTok provide powerful tools for creative impact.

When the focus is on detailed discussion or community

support, Reddit or specialized forums offer the depth and structure necessary. For rapid information sharing and public discourse, microblogging platforms excel. Conversely, private conversations and collaborative teamwork thrive best on messaging apps like WhatsApp and Discord.

For professionals and creatives seeking to build reputations or collaborate, niche networks offer targeted tools that mainstream platforms cannot replicate. Finally, when ideas demand elaboration and considered reading, blogging and publishing sites create spaces for sustained engagement.

By aligning platform choices with clear goals—whether to entertain, inform, connect, or collaborate—users maximize their social media effectiveness, leveraging the distinct strengths of each digital arena rather than falling prey to digital scatter. Social media is not one monolith but a suite of tailored environments; mastery lies in choosing the right stage for your voice.

1.4 Key Features of Social Media

Despite the diversity of platforms—ranging from microblogging sites like Twitter, photo-sharing worlds like Instagram, video-centric hubs like TikTok, to community-oriented networks such as Reddit and Facebook—certain features recur with remarkable consistency. These common elements are not happenstance but are carefully designed tools that guide how users interact, discover content, and ultimately how these networks thrive. They form the invisible architecture that sustains engagement and feeds the continuous cycle of content creation and consumption. Understanding these universal features offers insight into why social media feels simultaneously familiar and addictive, regardless of the platform.

Central to social media are *user profiles and bios*, the digital self-portraits that anchor every participant's presence. Profiles serve as identity hubs, combining a user's chosen name, photo, and a brief biography or description. This personalization is more than cosmetic: it conveys signals about who someone is— professionally, socially, or ideologically—effectively shaping first impressions and social connections. In this way, metadata embedded in profiles, such as location, interests, or links to other sites, helps machines and humans alike categorize users and tailor their experience. For instance, a musician's profile might attract fans, collaborators, and promoters, creating social and economic opportunities. The seemingly simple act of profile customization thus plays a pivotal role in constructing digital identities and fostering communities.

Another foundational feature is the *feed or timeline*—the central stream where users encounter content. The earliest social media platforms favored a purely chronological feed, presenting posts in the order they were published. This method feels straightforward and transparent; however, as the volume of content exploded, purely chronological timelines struggled to keep users engaged with relevant material. Enter the algorithmic feed: sophisticated software that curates and prioritizes content based on user behavior, preferences, and social connections. While these algorithms increase the likelihood of displaying engaging or meaningful posts, they also introduce challenges around transparency and filter bubbles. Nevertheless, both approaches embody a platform's fundamental goal: to guide users efficiently through vast oceans of information, nudging them to linger, react, and return.

Interaction metrics such as *reactions and engagement signals* are the heartbeat of social platforms. Likes, favorites, upvotes, hearts, and similar gestures serve dual functions. On one hand, they allow users to express approval, agreement, or amusement quickly and effortlessly. On the other, they provide critical feedback loops, influencing which content gains prominence. For example, a tweet with thousands of retweets and likes is more likely to appear on trending lists or be recommended to others. These simple clicks shape what becomes visible to millions, effectively crowd-sourcing editorial decisions. Yet, this reliance on engagement metrics can distort communication, incentivizing sensationalism or polarization to capture attention rather than nuanced discourse.

Complementing these are *commenting systems* that enable users to respond, debate, and elaborate. Comments transform social networks from broadcast arenas into interactive spaces fostering dialogue and community. Threaded replies help organize conversations, allowing for more coherent exchanges amid potential chaos. However, open commenting also necessitates *moderation policies* and community guidelines to combat abuse, misinformation, and harassment. Platforms employ a mix of automated filters, human moderators, and user reporting to maintain a balance between free expression and safe environments. The quality and rigor of moderation directly impact the health of online communities and the diversity of voices heard.

Closely linked to engagement is the capacity for *sharing and resharing*. The viral nature of social media hinges on how easily users can propagate content beyond their immediate circles. Sharing mechanisms—whether retweets, reposts, or "share" buttons—multiply the spread of ideas, images, and videos at unprecedented speeds.   This amplification can elevate previously obscure voices or cause misinformation to spiral out of control. Thus, sharing functions are double-edged swords: engines of democracy and connectivity, but also potential generators of echo chambers and social fragmentation.

The navigational ecosystem of social media relies heavily on *tags, mentions, and hashtags*—metadata tools that classify and connect content. Tags act like digital breadcrumbs, helping algorithms and users locate relevant posts through thematic labels.   Hashtags, popularized particularly by Twitter, have evolved into cultural signposts enabling users to join global conversations on events, social movements, or trends simply by adding a "#" prefix. Mentions, meanwhile, create direct connections between users, fostering dialogue and accountability. Together, these features transform individual posts into nodes of sprawling networks, organizing the immense flow of information into manageable and discoverable clusters.

Building on this, social media platforms often organize users into *groups, pages, and communities*.   These virtual spaces serve as formalized venues for public or private gatherings, united by common interests, goals, or identities.   Membership controls—ranging from open access to invitation-only—enable tailored social architectures: some groups aim for expansive outreach, while others prioritize intimacy and exclusivity. Facebook Groups, subreddit communities, and LinkedIn Pages exemplify how communities become foundational social units, shaping interactions and fostering trust or shared purpose beyond the frenzy of individual posts.

The vast scale of social platforms makes *search and discovery tools* indispensable. Keyword searches allow users to seek specific content or accounts, but the real innovation lies in recommendation algorithms that surface personalized suggestions based on past behavior and preferences. Trending topics highlight emergent phenomena, guiding collective attention toward real-time events, viral memes, or emergent social issues. These discovery features are vital for bridging the gap between an individual's existing network and the expansive universe of online content, sustaining user curiosity and platform vitality.

Amid these interactive layers, *privacy settings and controls* provide users with crucial agency over their digital footprint. Options for profile visibility, post audience restrictions, blocking, and data-sharing preferences give individuals the power to curate their experience and protect themselves from unwanted intrusion or exposure. As concerns about data misuse and surveillance grow, these tools become central to trust in social media and users' willingness to engage authentically. Platforms vary widely in the robustness and transparency of these controls, reflecting ongoing tensions between commercial interests and user rights.

To sustain engagement and encourage habitual use, social media platforms deploy *notifications and user alerts* that signal new interactions, updates, or recommended content. Push notifications, email alerts, and in-app badges serve as gentle reminders or urgent calls to action, drawing users back into the platform throughout the day. While effective, these features also raise questions about attention management and digital well-being, as constant pings risk fragmenting focus and contributing to compulsive behavior.

Finally, the design and functionality of social media

features are far from static; they undergo constant *evolution* driven by user behavior, technological innovation, and competitive dynamics. Platforms iterate on existing features—tweaking algorithms, introducing new content formats, or refining interface elements—to optimize engagement and user satisfaction. Sometimes, this results in unexpected consequences, such as the rise of Stories after Snapchat's success or the burgeoning popularity of short-form videos spurred by TikTok. This evolutionary process reflects an ongoing dialogue between platform designers and their communities, demonstrating how social media is a living system shaped by both creators and consumers.

Together, these key features form the scaffold upon which social media's dynamic and interconnected worlds are built. Their interplay governs how users express themselves, find meaning, and build relationships in the digital age. Recognizing these common threads enriches our understanding of why social media captivates millions and how it continues to transform social life globally.

1.5   Why People Use Social Media

Understanding why people engage with social media requires delving into a mosaic of motivations that overlap and often intertwine. At its core, social media serves as a versatile platform fulfilling a range of human needs and desires—social, informational, professional, and recreational. Each motivation represents a facet of the complex ways people seek connection, knowledge, expression, and enjoyment in an increasingly digital world.

Social connection and belonging lie at the heart of

social media's appeal. Humans are inherently social creatures, wired to seek companionship, affirmation, and community. Platforms like Facebook, Instagram, and WhatsApp act as modern gathering places where friendships are maintained, support networks nurtured, and collective identities strengthened. They offer a virtual "third place" beyond home and work where people can find camaraderie or empathy. This need for belonging can manifest as reconnecting with old friends, following communities that share opinions or experiences, or simply feeling part of a larger group— whether through local circles or global fandoms. In moments of isolation or stress, these connections can alleviate loneliness, offering both emotional comfort and a vital sense of human presence.

Alongside the desire for social connection is the impulse toward self-expression and identity construction. Social media platforms give individuals unprecedented tools to craft and project personal narratives. Through carefully chosen photos, status updates, and shared content, users engage in an ongoing process of impression management—shaping how they are seen by others and, perhaps more importantly, how they see themselves. This personal branding is evident not only among celebrities and influencers but also in everyday users exploring facets of their identity, experimenting with social roles, or building a reputation. Storytelling, whether through long posts or ephemeral stories, allows people to communicate values, aesthetics, humor, and experiences, turning social media into an evolving autobiography co-authored by audience feedback.

Beyond social needs, platforms have become indispensable sources of information and news. The traditional gatekeepers of news and knowledge have given way to a dynamic, decentralized flow of real-time updates.

Users turn to Twitter for breaking news, join specialized Facebook groups to access expert advice on niche topics, or follow journalists, scientists, and thought leaders for diverse perspectives. This shift democratizes information but also introduces challenges around accuracy and bias. Nonetheless, the immediacy of social media feeds satisfies an innate curiosity and the practical imperative to stay informed in a rapidly changing world. The user's role evolves from passive receiver to active participant—questioning, sharing, and sometimes contesting the newsworthiness of content.

Entertainment and leisure form another powerful incentive for social media use. Viral videos, memes, quizzes, and casual gaming embeds create spaces for lighthearted distraction and amusement. Platforms like TikTok and YouTube excel in delivering bite-sized content tailored to individual tastes, quickly satisfying desires for fun and relaxation. This entertainment function integrates seamlessly into daily routines— whether during a commute, a coffee break, or moments of downtime—transforming social media into a virtual playground that energizes and refreshes. The addictive potential of entertaining content also intersects with habitual use patterns, blurring the line between leisure and compulsion.

For many, especially in an era of digital economies and remote work, professional networking and development constitute a key motivation. Platforms such as LinkedIn offer virtual venues for job searches, industry networking, and skills exchange. Users can showcase portfolios, endorse colleagues, participate in professional groups, and stay abreast of sector trends. This form of social media engagement transcends casual interaction, positioning itself as a strategic tool for career advancement and lifelong learning. It reflects a broader shift where personal and professional identities increasingly intersect within digital spaces, enabling fluid boundary crossing between work, learning, and networking.

Creative content creation also drives engagement, empowering users to become artists, storytellers, and innovators in diverse media formats. Social media platforms provide accessible tools for producing and sharing art, videos, writing, music, and collaborative projects. They lower entry barriers to creative expression and foster communities of practice where critique, inspiration, and co-creation flourish. From amateur photographers to independent authors and hobbyist musicians, the availability of platforms like Instagram, YouTube, and TikTok has transformed social media into a global stage, where creativity is both a personal pursuit and a social act.

Interest-based and support communities embody another crucial function of social media. These groups— whether focused on health concerns, parenting, niche hobbies, or activism—offer peer advice, specialized knowledge, and solidarity. For example, forums dedicated to chronic illness provide emotional support and practical coping strategies, while fan clubs enable shared enthusiasm for media franchises. Such communities attest to social media's potential to connect fragmented or marginalized groups, building meaningful networks around common experiences or values that transcend geography and often, traditional social constraints.

Closely linked to social motivations is the pursuit of status and social capital. Accumulating followers, likes, endorsements, or shares acts as a currency of prestige and influence on many platforms. This social validation fosters feelings of accomplishment and recognition, motivating users to invest time and effort in content creation and engagement strategies. The metrics themselves—follower counts, reaction tallies, comments—function as tangible markers of success and popularity, influencing both individual identity and community dynamics. However, this quest for status can also induce pressure, competition, and performance anxiety, revealing the double-edged nature of social capital in online contexts.

An often underappreciated motivation behind social media use is compulsion, tied to the phenomenon known as Fear of Missing Out (FOMO). The constant stream of updates and notifications can trigger habits that feel less like voluntary engagement and more like behavioral addiction. Users frequently return to platforms not just out of desire but out of anxiety about being disconnected from social currents, events, or trending topics. This compulsion inflates the time invested in social media, sometimes undermining well-being, yet simultaneously reinforcing its central role in daily life. FOMO exemplifies the psychological interplay between human vulnerability and digital design, where need and habit coalesce.

Ultimately, these diverse motivations do not exist in isolation but operate in concert, shaping how and why individuals immerse themselves in social media environments. A single user's experience might move fluidly from seeking social reassurance to consuming news, from showcasing creative talents to professional networking, all within a single session. This synthesis reflects the multifaceted human needs that social media taps into—our desire for connection, knowledge, recognition, and enjoyment intertwined with the complexities of modern life. Recognizing this interplay deepens our understanding of social media not merely as a technological phenomenon but as a mirror and mold of contemporary human behavior.

1.6 The Digital Divide

The promise of social media is vast: connecting communities, amplifying voices, and democratizing information. Yet, this promise remains unevenly fulfilled because a significant portion of the global population lacks reliable access to digital platforms. This disparity is captured by the term *digital divide*, which refers to the gap between those with access to digital technologies, including devices and high-speed internet, and those without. The divide is particularly consequential in the realm of social media, where participation not only requires physical access but also the skills and resources to engage meaningfully. Understanding the digital divide uncovers why some individuals and communities remain digitally invisible, and why social media, despite its global reach, can reinforce existing inequalities rather than erase them.

At the heart of the digital divide lie infrastructure and connectivity barriers. While urban centers in many countries enjoy widespread broadband availability, large swaths of rural and underserved areas still struggle with unreliable or non-existent internet service. Even within connected regions, network speeds and stability vary greatly, limiting the user experience for those on slower connections. For instance, in parts of sub-Saharan Africa or rural Appalachia, intermittent service can make video streaming or participating in live social media chats frustrating or impossible. The cost and complexity of expanding fiber optic cables or 5G networks to remote locations also mean that infrastructure gaps persist despite technological advances. This uneven distribution creates a fundamental obstacle; without dependable connectivity, the doors to digital social spaces remain closed.

Device ownership presents another significant hurdle. Accessing social media platforms requires at minimum a smartphone, tablet, or computer—devices that may be prohibitively expensive for many. The cost barrier extends beyond the initial purchase to include maintenance, software updates, and data plans. For families with limited resources, prioritizing basic needs over technology is a harsh arithmetic. Moreover, hardware limitations can impede participation: older or second-hand devices may lack the processing power or storage required for modern social media apps, leading to slow performance or compatibility issues. The second-hand market, while helpful for affordability, often perpetuates disparities as those forced to rely on such devices face constrained digital experiences. Without affordable, capable hardware, access remains a patchwork rather than a pathway.

Beyond material barriers, socioeconomic and demographic factors shape who can participate online. Income level strongly predicts digital access; higher earners are more likely to own multiple devices and pay for premium internet services. Education influences familiarity with technology and confidence navigating digital environments. Age plays a dual role: younger generations, often called digital natives, tend to adopt social media effortlessly, while older adults may encounter apprehension or lack the required skills. Gender disparities also exist, especially in regions where cultural norms restrict women's autonomy and educational opportunities, limiting their digital access and expression. These intersecting factors mean the digital divide is not merely about technology but about structural inequalities that shape everyday lives.

Digital literacy compounds these issues—having a device and a connection is not enough if users lack the skills necessary to find, evaluate, and create content online. Competence ranges from basic tasks such as setting up accounts and managing privacy to critical abilities like identifying misinformation or engaging in respectful dialogue. Studies reveal stark differences in digital literacy levels, often correlated with age, education, and socioeconomic status. Without support to develop these skills, marginalized groups risk not only exclusion but also vulnerability to digital harms. Thus, digital literacy is both a gatekeeper and an enabler, determining whether individuals can transform access into meaningful participation.

The consequences of the digital divide ripple through social participation. When only some voices are amplified on social media, the broader democratic promise of these platforms is undermined. Communities lacking access or literacy remain underrepresented in public debates, civic discourse, and cultural exchanges. This skewed participation reinforces existing power dynamics and can entrench social isolation or misinformation. For example, during political elections or public health crises, those on the wrong side of the divide may miss critical updates or opportunities to influence outcomes. Digital inequalities thus translate into social inequalities, evidencing that the digital realm reflects, rather than transcends, offline realities.

Addressing the digital divide requires multi-faceted intervention strategies embracing governments, non-governmental organizations (NGOs), and the private sector. Public policy initiatives often focus on expanding broadband infrastructure through subsidies, public-private partnerships, and regulatory reforms aimed at increasing competition and lowering costs. NGOs complement these efforts by developing community training programs that enhance digital literacy and by distributing hardware to underserved populations. Technology companies bear a responsibility too, creating affordable devices, simplifying user experiences, and investing in connectivity projects as part of corporate social responsibility.   Effective strategies combine expanding physical access, lowering economic barriers, and fostering educational support, forming a holistic approach to inclusion.

Several real-world examples illustrate successful attempts to bridge the digital divide.   In India, the *Digital India* campaign significantly advanced rural broadband availability, while community centers provide shared internet access and training.   Kenya's *M-Pesa* platform transformed mobile technology into a tool for financial inclusion, empowering millions to engage digitally even with limited infrastructure.   In the United States, public libraries have become crucial access points for low-income residents, providing free internet and digital skills workshops.   These cases highlight the power of coordinated efforts that address the diverse obstacles to digital participation rather than treating the divide as a single problem.

Looking ahead, emerging solutions promise fresh ways to close gaps in connectivity and device access. Satellite internet, exemplified by initiatives like SpaceX's Starlink, aims to deliver high-speed connections to remote and underserved areas without relying on traditional ground-based infrastructure.   Community networks, which are locally owned and managed, foster grassroots digital inclusion tailored to specific needs and contexts.   Meanwhile, the development of low-cost smartphones and adaptive software focuses on affordability and usability for first-time users or those with limited digital experience. Such innovations reflect a growing recognition that closing the digital divide requires technological creativity alongside policy and educational commitment.

Reducing the digital divide involves weaving together infrastructure investment, economic support, skills development, and innovative technology. Equitable access to social media and the wider digital world is not merely a technical challenge but a social imperative. By overcoming physical, financial, and educational barriers, societies can move closer to the ideal of a truly inclusive digital public sphere—one where every individual's voice has the chance to be heard, and social media fulfills its promise as a tool for connection, empowerment, and participation.

Chapter 2

The Social Impact of Social Media

This chapter examines how social media reshapes human interaction, community life, identity formation, and collective behavior. We start by analyzing the transformation of interpersonal communication in digital contexts, then explore the dynamics of online community building. Next, we investigate individual identity and self-expression, followed by the dual effects of social platforms on personal relationships. We then turn to the mechanisms by which ideas and trends propagate online, and conclude by assessing how social media builds— or erodes—the social capital that underpins trust, reciprocity, and civic engagement.

2.1   Changing How We Communicate

For most of human history, communication was fundamentally a matter of being together—sharing space, gestures, and voices. The traditional modes of interaction, centered around face-to-face encounters and telephone conversations, established a rhythm and texture to human exchange that felt natural and immediate. Yet, in recent decades, a profound transformation has reshaped the terrain of communication, driven by the explosive rise of digital technologies. This shift moves us from purely vocal and physical presence toward a rich tapestry of multimedia social exchanges that unfold online, changing not only how we communicate but how we understand each other.

At the heart of this transformation lies the evolution of communication modes. Whereas early telephony extended voice over distances without losing the real-time essence of conversation, digital platforms expanded modes beyond voice to include written text, images, video, and integrated multimedia experiences. Initially, interactions replicated the telephone's immediacy by enabling synchronous exchanges—instant messaging or video calls that preserve back-and-forth dialogue. However, the advent of social media introduced asynchronous communication channels where postings, comments, and messages need not be responded to immediately and can persist indefinitely. This duality profoundly alters conversational dynamics; asynchronous formats allow reflection, wider participation, and a more curated presentation of self, but they also blur temporal boundaries, complicating expectations for response and engagement.

Synchronous and asynchronous modes, then, coexist and complement one another in the digital landscape. Real-time interactions like video chats or live streams mimic the directness of earlier communication but with added visual richness. In contrast, asynchronous exchanges via posts, forums, and threaded comments offer flexibility, letting participants absorb and reply at their convenience. Social platforms often blend these modes, enabling a user to comment later on a live broadcast or to switch from a public timeline post to a private messaging thread, illustrating an ever more intricate web of communication possibilities.

This complexity extends into the varied public and

private channels now available. Traditional face-to-face exchanges were generally private or confined to small groups. Digital communication, however, spans from highly public 'timelines' or feeds accessible to broad audiences, to closed groups formed around shared interests, and direct messages reserved for intimate conversations. Each setting carries distinct social rules and privacy implications. Public posts invite broad visibility and interaction, sometimes fostering community but also exposing participants to scrutiny or misunderstanding. Closed groups create spaces for more trusted exchanges, while direct messaging channels are the digital equivalent of whispered conversations. Navigating these layers requires new literacies around audience, context, and personal boundaries—skills less necessary when all communication was localized and ephemeral.

Crucially, multimedia integration enriches these digital dialogues. Text alone gives way to a vibrant ensemble of images, audio snippets, video clips, and live streams. This mix allows for far more expressive and nuanced communication. For instance, a text post announcing a life event gains emotional depth when accompanied by a photograph or a short video. Live streaming introduces a form of shared immediacy—viewers react in real time through comments and digitally mediated applause. Such multimedia creates a sensory experience that more closely approximates in-person communication's richness, while also enabling new forms of creativity and storytelling. The result is a language of communication that is less linear and more layered, inviting participants to engage multiple senses and interpret meaning through diverse modes simultaneously.

Non-verbal cues, once limited to facial expressions, tone

of voice, and body language, have found new digital forms. Emojis, GIFs, stickers, and reaction buttons serve as shorthand to convey emotion, tone, or social nuance in ways that plain text cannot. A smiling emoji can soften criticism, a GIF can inject humor or sarcasm, and a 'like' button can acknowledge without interrupting conversation flow. These elements compensate for the absence of physical presence, filling gaps in expression and helping mitigate miscommunication. However, they also introduce a new semiotic system with its own rules and cultural variability. What may be an innocent sticker in one community could carry a different meaning elsewhere, demanding users learn these evolving codes to communicate effectively and empathetically.

Alongside these changes, the language of digital communication has developed its own character and grammar. Internet slang, abbreviations, memes, and hashtags have become integral tools for expressing identity, humor, and social commentary. Memes, in particular, function as compact cultural artifacts— visual or textual—that spread rapidly and mutate through shared understanding, often layering irony and community-specific references. Hashtags organize discourse and amplify voices across dispersed networks, while abbreviations like 'LOL' or 'BRB' condense common phrases to streamline interaction. This emergent internet language reflects the dynamic, playful nature of online communication and showcases how users creatively adapt language to fit new contexts and technologies.

Message persistence versus ephemerality presents another dimension to this communication shift. Unlike spoken words, digital messages often linger indefinitely—the permanence of posts and comments can preserve conversations and memories for years. This endurance influences behavior; people may craft messages more carefully, aware they could be resurfaced. Yet, the rise of ephemeral modes, such as 'stories' that disappear after 24 hours, introduces a sense of urgency and spontaneity reminiscent of face-to-face interaction's fleeting nature. These disappearing messages encourage candidness and reduce pressure for permanence, but also shift the focus toward momentary sharing and rapid consumption. The interplay between lasting and transient content reflects broader cultural tensions around privacy, self-presentation, and the desire to memorialize versus move on.

In this ocean of communication streams, information overload and the attention economy become defining challenges. Platforms generate rapid-fire notifications and an unending flow of updates, fragmenting attention and leading to fatigue or disengagement. Users develop coping strategies, such as muting notifications, curating friend lists, or employing specialized apps to regain focus. Meanwhile, platforms compete fiercely for user attention, designing interfaces and algorithms to maximize engagement. The result is a tug-of-war between human cognitive limits and technological possibilities, making digital literacy not only a matter of content understanding but also of managing one's own attentional resources.

As communication moves online, digital etiquette and social norms evolve alongside technology. What counts as polite, respectful, or disruptive changes as the venue changes. Rules around response times, tone, and content vary from platform to platform and across cultures. Practices like 'thread hijacking,' oversharing, or 'lurking' (observing without engaging) have come under scrutiny, while new etiquette encourages clarity, empathy, and awareness of diverse audiences. These shifting norms show that the digital space is both a social laboratory and a contested field, where communities negotiate boundaries of acceptable behavior and strive toward more constructive interactions.

Taken together, these changes have fundamentally redefined the pace, style, and reach of human conversation. Communication is no longer confined by geography or immediate presence; it is now a dynamic, multi-channeled, and multimedia-rich flow that unfolds across public and private spheres in real time and over extended periods. The result is a more complex environment where identity, emotion, and information intermingle in novel ways, offering unprecedented opportunities for connection—and raising fresh questions about privacy, authenticity, and attention. As we continue navigating this evolving landscape, understanding the mechanics and meanings of digital communication remains indispensable to making sense of our contemporary social world.

2.2 Building Online Communities

At its most basic, an online community is more than just a scattered group of internet users navigating the same platform; it is a constellation of connections, shared purposes, and mutual recognition that transform individuals into a collective. What turns a set of users into a coherent online community is the interplay of interaction, common interests or identities, and a sense of belonging. This transformation hinges on sustained communication, shared norms, and the infrastructure that supports meaningful engagement. Rather than mere aggregation, communities embody cohesion—users recognize themselves as part of a group with collective experiences and often common goals.

A useful way to understand online communities is to distinguish between those formed around shared interests and those rooted in shared identities. Interest-based communities emerge because members enjoy the same hobbies or pursuits—think of photography enthusiasts uniting on Instagram, or fans dissecting favorite TV shows on Reddit. These groups thrive on the exchange of knowledge, tips, and experiences related to a particular subject. In contrast, identity-based communities revolve around intrinsic or social aspects of the members' selves, such as cultural heritage, gender, sexual orientation, or professional affiliation. For example, online forums for LGBTQ+ youth or diaspora networks foster connection through shared lived experiences and challenges, often offering vital social support and solidarity. While interest groups may be more open-ended and fluid, identity-based communities often serve as sanctuaries and sources of empowerment, where members find validation and collective voice.

The tone, safety, and trajectory of these communities are largely shaped by moderators and administrators—those who serve as gatekeepers and rule-makers. Far from mere arbiters of content, moderators cultivate the space's culture. By enforcing guidelines, mediating disputes, and supporting productive dialogue, they set the conditions for trust and inclusivity. On platforms like Discord or Facebook Groups, moderators might ban trolls or remove harmful posts, ensuring the space remains respectful and aligned with the community's ethos. The authority they wield is crucial but delicate; too heavy-handed, and it stifles spontaneity; too lax, and the group risks fragmentation or toxicity. Effective moderation balances firmness with empathy, cultivating a place where diverse voices can coexist without descending into chaos.

The emergence of community norms—shared expectations about behavior—and governance structures often starts informally. Over time, as members interact and respond to challenges, guidelines naturally crystallize. These can range from explicit written rules to unspoken rituals and etiquette. Platforms themselves may provide frameworks for governance: for instance, subreddit moderators collaborate to draft policies that evolve in response to new forms of misuse or changing member attitudes. Importantly, governance is adaptive; norms shift as the group matures, reflecting evolving values, priorities, and social contexts. This dynamic system of rules and enforcement shapes not only the participants' conduct but also their sense of ownership and responsibility, reinforcing the social fabric that binds the community.

Platform affordances—the technological tools and features available—play an outsized role in fostering cohesion. Features like groups, channels, or dedicated forums create bounded spaces that signal belonging. Event scheduling tools, tagging systems, and threaded conversations help members stay organized and engaged. For example, Slack channels enable teams to segment conversations by topic, while Facebook's "Events" feature facilitates planning virtual meetups or webinars, cementing communal bonds through shared experiences. Furthermore, features like reaction emojis, badges, and profile customization allow individuals to express identity within the group's framework, deepening their connection. These design choices scaffold interactions, turning loose networks into more structured and lasting social units.

Sustaining engagement requires rituals and recurring

activities that capture attention and invite participation. Online communities thrive when members anticipate regular events or campaigns—a weekly photo challenge, monthly live Q&A sessions, or hashtag movements celebrating shared causes. These rituals provide rhythm and predictability, essential ingredients for ongoing involvement. The seemingly simple act of rallying around a hashtag, such as #BlackLivesMatter or #MeToo, illustrates how digital campaigns can amplify voices and galvanize global solidarity. Virtual meetups, gaming nights, and skill workshops further reinforce cohesion, blending social interaction with personal enrichment. These engagement strategies transform passive observers into active contributors and strengthen communal identity through shared experiences.

It is within these continually negotiated interactions that a powerful sense of belonging and collective identity takes root. Shared symbols—logos, slogans, or memes—alongside specialized language or inside jokes act as markers of membership. These cultural artifacts foster group solidarity by making members feel seen and understood by their peers. Collective identity also arises from aligning around common goals or values, whether it's advocating for environmental action, celebrating niche fandoms, or providing mutual aid. This psychological sense of "we-ness" enhances commitment and resilience, especially when communities face external challenges or internal conflicts. As members internalize the group's narrative, they contribute not just content but a piece of themselves, enriching the community fabric.

Like all social organisms, online communities experience life cycles. They begin with formation—the early phase marked by enthusiastic founding members who define purpose and norms. Growth follows as new members join, expanding diversity and complexity. Maturity arrives when the group establishes stable routines, governance, and a broad shared identity. However, communities can also decline, as member interest wanes, leadership fizzles, or conflicts arise. Decline need not be fatal; many communities find ways to revitalize themselves through rebranding, introducing new leadership, or pivoting focus. Understanding this life cycle helps communities anticipate challenges and craft strategies to endure or reinvent themselves, adapting to shifting digital landscapes.

One of the most intriguing distinctions within communities is between *bonding* and *bridging* ties. Bonding ties are the close-knit, intense relationships that provide emotional support and deepen trust—akin to family or close friends. These are common in identity-based groups or support communities where vulnerability and mutual aid are paramount. Bridging ties, by contrast, connect disparate groups and individuals, serving as bridges across social divides. They are crucial in broader networks where diversity and new information flow freely. For instance, a large hobby forum may foster bridging ties between different subcultures, enabling cross-pollination of ideas. Healthy online ecosystems often balance both: bonding for depth and support, bridging for innovation and reach.

Beyond social connection, communities wield collective power through mobilization. Digital platforms make organizing activism, fundraising, and awareness campaigns more accessible and visible than ever. Online groups have coordinated protests, launched crowdfunding efforts, and disseminated critical information across geographies and demographics with remarkable speed and scale. The Arab Spring uprisings, global climate strikes, and various humanitarian drives illustrate how digital communities can transform shared values into coordinated action. Mobilization amplifies the voice and impact of marginalized or dispersed populations, turning virtual solidarity into tangible change. It also requires strategic leadership, communication, and trust—qualities cultivated through the social infrastructure outlined earlier.

The dynamics of building and sustaining online communities ultimately hinge on a delicate balance of structure and spontaneity, governance and freedom, bonding and bridging. Successful communities craft inclusive identities and resilient norms, supported by thoughtful moderation and platform tools. Engagement rituals and shared symbols deepen belonging, while awareness of lifecycle stages guides adaptation. Whether an intimate support group or a sprawling global movement, thriving online communities are those that nurture participation, respond to members' evolving needs, and unlock the transformative power of collective human connection in the digital age.

2.3 Social Identity and Self-Expression

In the sprawling realm of social media, identity is both crafted and performed with a careful blend of intention and spontaneity. Users are no longer passive consumers but active architects of their digital selves—designing profiles, curating content, and navigating a complex social landscape where personal and group identities intersect visibly and vividly.

At the foundation of this digital self-construction lies the profile: the homepage of one's online persona. Profiles, consisting of elements like bios, avatars, usernames, and handles, serve as shorthand signals to the world. A succinct bio can reveal interests, values, affiliations, or humor; an avatar, whether a polished photograph or a stylized illustration, projects mood and aesthetic sensibility. Handles, especially on platforms like Twitter or Instagram, function as verbal signatures that may incorporate real names, nicknames, or coded references to insider group memberships. Together, these components act as the building blocks of identity performance, offering the first impression in social interactions and laying the groundwork for deeper social engagement.

But profiles are only the stage. Self-presentation strategies unfold through the ongoing selection and arrangement of posted content. Impression management—a concept borrowed from sociologist Erving Goffman—helps explain how users consciously or unconsciously control what others see to influence perceptions. Content curation, for example, involves choosing which photos, updates, or shared articles to display, often emphasizing achievements, cultural tastes, or personal milestones. Many individuals extend this process into brand storytelling: a deliberate narrative arc that shapes their social media presence into something cohesive, relatable, or aspirational. Influencers and professionals, for instance, frequently weave personal anecdotes with polished visuals to forge connections and cultivate followers. This strategy turns profile pages into carefully choreographed identities tailored for particular audiences.

Yet, the arena of digital self-expression also contends with varying degrees of transparency and anonymity. Different platforms adopt diverse policies that profoundly shape user behavior. Environments encouraging faceless participation—such as anonymous forums or pseudonymous chat rooms—offer freedom from real-world identity constraints, allowing for experimentation or candid discourse without social repercussion. Conversely, platforms mandating real-name policies, like Facebook's initial design, emphasize authenticity and verifiability, aiming to reduce trolling and enhance accountability. This dichotomy creates distinct modes of interaction: the masked versus the unmasked self, each with its own affordances and limitations. Users must decide how much of their true identity to reveal, balancing the desire for expression against privacy concerns and social expectations.

This leads to an ongoing tension between curated personas and authenticity. On one hand, users strive to present an idealized version of themselves—a polished, attractive, or successful identity crafted for public consumption. On the other, there is an increasing cultural premium on "keeping it real," sharing raw, often vulnerable aspects that foster trust and emotional connection. However, authenticity in social media is seldom absolute; it is performative in itself, selectively disclosing aspects of the self that conform to social norms or personal comfort. This dialectic fuels debates around whether social media encourages genuine self-expression or perpetuates façades. In truth, many users oscillate between these modes, negotiating a digital middle ground that is both personalized and socially acceptable.

Sharing personal details publicly is a double-edged sword, introducing privacy trade-offs. Disclosing intimate or identifying information can enhance social bonds, invite support, and build community. Yet, it also exposes users to risks such as identity theft, stalking, or professional repercussions, especially when sensitive content circulates widely beyond the original intent. Semi-public spheres, like private groups or ephemeral stories, attempt to mediate this by restricting visibility, but digital traces often persist unpredictably. Thus, users constantly calibrate what to reveal, weighing the social benefits against the potential personal costs—a negotiation central to the digital self.

Complicating matters further is the multiplicity of online selves people maintain. Across diverse platforms—LinkedIn, Instagram, TikTok, Reddit—individuals often present distinct facets of identity matched to the platform's norms and audiences. A person might appear as a professional expert on LinkedIn, a lifestyle enthusiast on Instagram, and a witty, irreverent commentator on Reddit. These partitioned selves serve functional and psychological purposes: they allow users to explore different aspects of their personality and maintain boundaries between social roles. But they can also impose organizational challenges, requiring constant management to ensure coherence or prevent inadvertent overlaps.

Integral to this dynamic is the impact of feedback on digital self-esteem. Likes, comments, shares, and follower counts are not mere metrics; they function as social currency influencing users' perceptions of self-worth and social belonging. Positive feedback can boost confidence, encourage further engagement, and help establish a valued identity within online communities. Conversely, negative or absent feedback may trigger self-doubt, anxiety, or withdrawal. This feedback loop shapes behavior, sometimes intensifying efforts at self-presentation or prompting strategic modifications to content in pursuit of approval. The emotional stakes tied to validation underscore the psychological complexity underpinning social media use.

However, managing multiple identities and seeking validation can lead to identity fragmentation and conflict. When distinct personas clash—say, a conservative professional image contradicting a more avant-garde personal expression—users may experience cognitive dissonance, feeling torn between competing demands and values. This tension can cause stress or feelings of inauthenticity, particularly when real-world and online identities diverge sharply. For some, reconciling these facets requires compartmentalization or careful audience management; for others, it can prompt transformative redefinitions of self. Digital life thus introduces novel pressures to integrate diverse selves into a coherent identity narrative.

Adding another layer, community norms and peer feedback exert strong influence on self-concept. Social groups—whether fandoms, professional circles, or activist networks—establish shared values, language, and aesthetic codes that members learn and emulate. Acceptance often depends on conforming to these norms, shaping how individuals express themselves and which identities they emphasize. Conversely, communities can also foster experimentation and innovation, encouraging users to explore alternative identities or challenge mainstream narratives. The interplay between individual agency and collective influence highlights the social construction of identity within digital environments.

Taken together, these forces illustrate how social media serves as both a toolkit and a stage for identity work. It empowers users with unprecedented means of self-expression and social connection, yet simultaneously imposes constraints through norms, algorithms, and surveillance. The identities we project online are never fixed but continually negotiated, fragmented, and reshaped in response to feedback and context. Understanding these dynamics requires appreciating the delicate performance, experimentation, and adaptation inherent in every post, profile update, and interaction. In this evolving digital theatre, social identity is both the product and the process of self-expression, mediated by technology and human creativity alike.

2.4 Strengthening and Weakening Relationships

Social platforms have redefined how we maintain, forge, and sometimes fracture our interpersonal bonds. They act as both bridges and barriers, amplifying human connection while also introducing novel pressures and vulnerabilities. Understanding these dual roles requires examining the nuanced ways digital environments influence relationships, from the daily routines of messaging to the shadows cast by unseen hostility.

- **Maintaining Existing Ties**

  At their best, social platforms serve as tools for sustaining friendships that might otherwise fade under the weight of distance and busy lives. Messaging apps and instant notifications create an effortless rhythm of communication that mimics casual in-person encounters—a quick text, a shared meme, a birthday wish—which together weave a continuous social fabric. News feeds serve not only as information conduits but as ongoing social diaries, where updates on career milestones, family events, and personal triumphs create touchpoints for engagement and empathy. Sharing photos, videos, and articles enhances this dynamic, providing glimpses into daily experiences that deepen relational intimacy even without physical proximity. In this way, digital platforms can scaffold friendships by lowering barriers to contact and reinforcing emotional presence.

- **Reconnecting Distant Acquaintances**

  Beyond reinforcing close bonds, social media also enables the rediscovery of long-lost connections— the acquaintances we once knew but who slipped into the background of life. These "weak ties" are often overlooked yet hold surprising social capital. Sociologist Mark Granovetter highlighted their importance decades ago: such loose connections bring fresh information, new perspectives, and diverse opportunities that strong ties may lack. Platforms like Facebook or LinkedIn facilitate the serendipitous encounter with former classmates, distant cousins, or old colleagues, rekindling networks that serve as professional conduits or casual social lifelines. While these rediscoveries rarely blossom into intense friendships, they enrich our social tapestry by providing a reservoir of social resources and a sense of belonging to a larger community.

- **Forming New Connections**

  The art of making new friends is simultaneously simpler and more complex online. Algorithm-driven friend suggestions and "People You May Know" features tap into shared affiliations, mutual contacts, or geographical proximity to propose potential connections. This can accelerate network growth but also subtly guide social diversification in curated directions. Friend

49

requests and follower dynamics allow users to establish varied relationships: some reciprocal and intimate, others asymmetrical and distant. Unlike traditional introduction settings, these connections often begin without physical cues, requiring new norms of trust and verification. Yet, this digital terrain opens doors to communities of interest, enabling individuals to connect around niche hobbies, political causes, or cultural identities in ways unbounded by geography. However, the quality of new relationships varies widely, reminding us that quantity alone does not equal meaningful social capital.

- **Parasocial Bonds**

  Social platforms have also given rise to parasocial relationships—one-sided emotional attachments to influencers, celebrities, or content creators who remain largely unaware of individual followers. These bonds blur the lines between audience and participant, often driven by frequent exposure to curated personas and intimate storytelling formats like vlogs or live streams. Parasocial interactions can provide comfort, inspiration, and a sense of companionship, especially in contexts of isolation or loneliness. However, they also risk reinforcing illusions of friendship and creating emotional dependencies unreciprocated in reality. As followers invest affective energy without mutual exchange, these relationships raise questions about authenticity and the emotional labor entailed in digital stardom.

- **Online Social Support**

  On a more positive note, digital platforms have revolutionized social support by transcending barriers of time, space, and stigma. Peer counseling groups, online forums, and moderated communities offer vital spaces where individuals facing health challenges, grief, or marginalized identities find validation and advice. Anonymity and accessibility make these virtual arenas uniquely valuable for those reluctant to seek traditional help. Particularly during crises—such as the COVID-19 pandemic—online communities became lifelines, facilitating collective resilience and resource sharing. Yet, the effectiveness of such support depends on careful moderation and the fostering of genuine empathy, illustrating how technology amplifies human compassion when thoughtfully deployed.

- **Harassment, Trolling, and Cyberbullying**

  Yet these digital landscapes are not utopias. Harassment, trolling, and cyberbullying constitute dark undercurrents that compromise the safety and well-being of many users. The relative anonymity and disinhibition of online spaces embolden behaviors rarely expressed face-to-face. Targeted attacks—ranging from cruel comments to coordinated campaigns of abuse—inflict psychological harm, damaging self-esteem and even precipitating mental health crises. Studies consistently reveal high prevalence rates across age groups, with young people particularly vulnerable. Social platforms grapple with the challenge of balancing free expression and protection, often under public scrutiny for inadequate responses. This persistent negativity illustrates how technological mediation can escalate social conflict and erode interpersonal trust.

- **Privacy, Surveillance, and Trust Erosion**

  Privacy concerns further complicate the relational dynamics within social media. Friend monitoring and the ease of digital surveillance—whether sanctioned or surreptitious—introduce ambiguity and suspicion into personal exchanges. Users may discover themselves subject to constant observation, from innocuous "likes" to more intrusive data mining handled by platform owners or third parties. This visibility alters behavior, fostering performative interactions and self-censorship. Moreover, the misuse or unauthorized sharing of personal information can betray relational trust, turning once-safe spaces into arenas of vulnerability. Such breaches ripple beyond individual harm, undermining collective confidence in social networks and prompting broader societal debates over digital ethics and regulation.

- **Ghosting and Relationship Decay**

  The digital era has also birthed new forms of relational disengagement, notably ghosting—sudden, unexplained silence replacing previous communication. Unlike face-to-face withdrawal, ghosting leaves the affected party without closure, incubating confusion and hurt. Gradual fading, whereby interactions steadily diminish until a connection becomes dormant, likewise proliferates in online settings where low friction permits easy disengagement. These patterns reflect both the convenience and cruelty of mediated relationships, revealing how connection can be as fleeting as a click. Over time, the accumulation of such dissolutions subtly reshapes social norms around commitment and accountability.

- **Balancing Online/Offline Boundaries**

  Given these complexities, managing the boundary between online and offline social life emerges as a vital skill. Conscious regulation of screen time, selective sharing of personal information, and intentional digital detoxes help preserve mental health and relational integrity. Establishing clear norms about availability and response expectations can mitigate misunderstandings and emotional exhaustion. Importantly, offline interactions continue to anchor trust and emotional depth in ways that online communication alone struggles to replicate. A mindful balance recognizes the strengths of digital connectivity without allowing it to displace the richer texture of embodied, face-to-face encounters.

In aggregate, social platforms wield immense power to both strengthen and strain human relationships. They ease maintenance of existing ties, enable rediscovery of distant acquaintances, and unlock pathways to new connections otherwise unimaginable. Simultaneously, they incubate parasocial attachments, nurture communities of support, and expose users to damaging harassment and privacy risks. Relationship deterioration takes on new digital forms, while the challenge of balancing virtual and real-world interactions becomes ever more pressing. Navigating this landscape demands awareness of the complex interplay between technology and human psychology— a reminder that social media is neither inherently hostile nor benevolent, but a mirror reflecting the best and worst of our social nature.

2.5 Spreading Ideas and Trends

At the heart of how ideas, trends, and information ripple through society lies the intricate web of human connections coupled with technological channels. Understanding this interplay sheds light on why some content catches fire while other messages sputter and fade. Central to this is the concept of *information diffusion*, where ideas spread much like rumors or epidemics, traversing a network of individuals through sharing behaviors, social ties, and interactive platforms.

Models of information diffusion borrow insights from epidemiology and network science, envisioning ideas as contagious entities passed along social links. Each person exposed to a piece of content faces a choice: to adopt and share it further or not. The probability of passing on an idea depends not only on personal interest but also on the influence of the source and the perceived credibility of the message. As information cascades through these branching chains, patterns emerge—sometimes broad but shallow, sometimes narrow yet deep—shaping the overall reach and impact.

These diffusion patterns are deeply shaped by *network effects*—the structural properties of the social fabric itself. A densely connected community, where individuals share many mutual contacts, can accelerate spread due to frequent reinforcement and trust, fostering what sociologists call *clustering*. When shared repeatedly within tight-knit groups, content gains social validation, further boosting its viral potential. Moreover, *cascades* occur when one share triggers a chain reaction, revitalizing the momentum across otherwise unconnected parts of the network. The interplay of user density, clustering, and cascade effects thus forms a fertile ground for rapid proliferation.

Within these networks, certain individuals hold outsized power in influencing trends. These *influencers* or *super-spreaders* possess broad reach—whether through celebrity, expertise, or sheer connectivity—and act as amplifiers of messages. By sharing content, they inject visibility into previously uncharted circles. Their endorsement often shapes public perception, serving as a shortcut for others to judge a message's worthiness. The phenomenon reveals a curious mix of trust and spotlight: while many receive information through mundane peer-to-peer exchange, key nodes in the network can ignite widespread attention by harnessing their platform, followers, or reputation.

Cultural formats such as *memes*, viral *challenges*, and *hashtag activism* crystallize this process into participatory rituals. Memes—those playful, image-text hybrids—distill complex ideas into instantly recognizable symbols, inviting endless creative remixing. Challenges, whether dance routines or fundraising pushes, encourage collective action by lowering barriers to engagement and infusing fun. Hashtag activism, meanwhile, harnesses a simple tagging mechanism to aggregate awareness, spotlight issues, and coordinate dispersed efforts. These affordances facilitate rapid participation by making content easy to replicate and adapt, transforming solitary viewers into active contributors.

Yet the momentum of viral content rarely relies on human participants alone; behind the scenes lurk *algorithmic curation systems* that select, prioritize, and amplify certain stories over others. Platforms like Facebook, Twitter, TikTok, and Instagram employ complex recommendation engines and trending feeds designed to maximize engagement. These algorithms analyze user behavior—clicks, likes, shares, watch time—and dynamically tailor content streams. While this personalization can connect people with relevant material, it also tends to magnify popular content rapidly, sometimes producing feedback loops that favor sensational or emotionally charged material. The invisible hand of algorithms decisively shapes what messages gain prominence and which languish unseen.

This mechanism ties directly into the psychological undercurrents of *emotional contagion* and *social proof*, which form powerful social drivers of sharing. Humans are innately wired to respond to emotions expressed by others; content evoking joy, anger, fear, or awe triggers empathetic reactions that enhance virality. Meanwhile, *social proof*—the phenomenon where people look to others' behavior to guide their own—fuels the compulsion to join in sharing what appears popular or endorsed by trusted peers. Together, these forces create a fertile feedback environment, where emotional resonance and visible peer support combine to propel a message far beyond its origin.

Harnessing these dynamics is the domain of *rapid mobilization and online campaigns*, where viral spread becomes a tool for social action. Digital activism channels—from grassroots petition drives to crowdfunding efforts—leverage the speed and reach of social media to galvanize support and amplify causes. Viral campaigns can raise awareness on global issues, trigger mass protests, or swiftly generate funds for emergencies. The ease of participation, combined with emotionally compelling calls to action, gives these campaigns unprecedented power to reshape public discourse and policy debates in real time.

However, the same mechanisms that enable positive virality also expose vulnerabilities, especially in the realm of *misinformation and rumor dynamics*. False or misleading content can exploit network structures and psychological tendencies to spread widely, often faster than verified facts. Misinformation tends to thrive when sensationalism meets algorithmic amplification and users' confirmation biases. Once entrenched, rumors distort public understanding and can erode trust. The speed at which falsehoods spread creates urgent challenges for societies striving to manage information quality in an age of instant communication.

In response, *content moderation and fact-checking* efforts have become central to many platforms and civic institutions. Automated filters, human moderators, and third-party verification organizations work to identify and curb harmful or deceptive material. Meanwhile, community-driven corrections—through comments, rebuttals, and expert annotations—play a vital role in crowd-sourcing truth. Though imperfect and often contested, these interventions reflect the ongoing attempt to balance free expression with the need to maintain a trustworthy informational landscape amid the torrent of content.

Collectively, the viral spread of ideas and trends rests on a complex synergy of human behavior, social structures, technological design, and cultural creativity. The interplay of connection patterns, influential actors, participatory formats, emotional resonance, algorithmic choices, and vigilant moderation shapes whether a spark ignites a wildfire or quietly fizzles out. Recognizing these multifaceted forces not only deepens our understanding of how information moves but also equips us to navigate and shape the ever-evolving currents of communication in the digital age.

2.6   Social Media and Social Capital

At the heart of understanding how social media reshapes human interaction lies the concept of *social capital*—the resources embedded in networks of interpersonal relationships, enabling individuals and groups to achieve goals they might struggle to reach alone. Social scientists often classify social capital into three interrelated types: *bonding*, *bridging*, and *linking* capital. Bonding social capital refers to the close, emotionally intense connections among family and close friends that provide strong support and solidarity.   Bridging social capital, by contrast, encompasses more distant, heterogeneous ties that link diverse social groups, facilitating the exchange of novel information and broader worldviews.   Linking social capital extends these connections vertically across institutional or power hierarchies, connecting individuals or groups with formal authorities and resources beyond their immediate social spheres.   Together, these forms of capital underpin trust, reciprocity, and collective action—essential ingredients for vibrant communities and effective societal functioning.

Online spaces have remixed these classical categories, altering the scale, speed, and texture of social ties. Bonding ties persist in digital format as private groups, direct messages, and family chats flourish, enabling moments of personal support and intimate sharing.   Yet, bridging ties arguably flourish more visibly online: platforms like Twitter, Instagram, and Reddit foster loose connections across geography, culture, and ideology. These distant networks can expose users to new ideas and mobilize support around common causes, often at an unprecedented scale. Linking capital also finds expression in online interactions that connect citizens to policymakers via digital petitions, live-streamed town halls, and advocacy groups harnessing hashtag campaigns to translate grassroots voices into political influence. The digital transformation of social capital therefore invites us to rethink how fast, flitting online interactions might build—or erode—the deeper reservoirs of trust and cooperation necessary for societal well-being.

To grasp the health of social capital in digital environments, researchers have developed various metrics transcending simple counts of friends or followers. Network size remains a baseline measure, but engagement frequency—how often users interact through comments, shares, and likes—offers richer insights into relationship strength. Mutual exchange, such as responding with support or information, signals reciprocity and trust, serving as a currency of goodwill in online communities. More nuanced indicators track the diversity of connections, distinguishing bonding from bridging capital, and assess the flow of resources like advice, emotional support, or professional referrals. For instance, an active LinkedIn user who both mentors peers and receives career guidance exemplifies digital social capital's reciprocal dynamics. Taken together, these metrics illuminate how digital social networks constitute valuable, though complex and often fragile, social ecosystems.

Social media's potential to accelerate professional networking and mentorship vividly illustrates the practical utility of digital social capital. Platforms like LinkedIn, Twitter, and emerging niche communities enable users to showcase skills, seek advice, and forge connections beyond traditional geographical or institutional boundaries. By lowering barriers to mentorship, they democratize access to knowledge and career opportunities for many who might otherwise remain excluded. Digital mentorship often unfolds asymmetrically—experts share guidance with novices in ways that feel immediate and personalized—yet happens at scale, fostering vibrant peer-to-peer learning cultures. Such interactions reinforce linking capital by bridging individuals with influential actors and resources crucial for professional growth. However, this potential is not uniform; differences in digital literacy, network composition, and platform norms shape who benefits most, underscoring deeper questions about equity in the digital age.

The civic sphere has been particularly transformed by the emergence of social media as a platform for collective action and public deliberation. Online petitions rapidly gather signatures, while crowdfunding campaigns mobilize resources for social causes, often generating awareness among millions of users globally. Hashtag movements like #MeToo and #BlackLivesMatter leverage wide-reaching networks to amplify marginalized voices and catalyze offline protests, legislative reforms, or corporate accountability. Social media also hosts deliberative forums where citizens debate policies, share news, and negotiate solutions, albeit accompanied by challenges of misinformation and polarization. These digitally fueled dynamics exemplify how social media expands both the reach and speed of civic engagement, potentially revitalizing democratic participation but also requiring careful attention to sustaining trust and meaningful dialogue.

Central to the sustenance of social capital online are the intertwined norms of trust, reciprocity, and resource exchange. When users share timely information, emotional support, or practical advice, they reinforce the implicit social contracts that bind communities together. This mutual exchange engenders reputational capital: individuals who consistently provide valuable contributions often gain credibility, leading others to invest time and effort into the relationship. Such trust enables collective problem-solving and facilitates coordinated action, from organizing neighborhood cleanups to supporting disaster relief efforts. Conversely, the absence or breakdown of trust—manifested in trolling, misinformation, or performative gestures—can quickly deplete social capital, leaving communities fragmented and less resilient.

Yet the ability to build and benefit from digital social capital is unequally distributed. Access to reliable internet, digital devices, and user-friendly platforms forms the baseline of opportunity, but beyond hardware, digital literacy—the skill to navigate, critically evaluate, and engage with online content—profoundly shapes participation quality. Furthermore, individuals' network positions matter; highly connected users or "influencers" wield disproportionate social capital, while peripheral users may struggle to be heard or access valuable exchanges. These disparities reflect and reinforce wider social inequalities, creating capital gaps that can limit social mobility and civic participation. Recognizing these structural challenges is essential for designing inclusive digital environments where social capital can flourish equitably.

Given these complexities, several strategies can enhance social capital in online settings. Prioritizing meaningful interaction over sheer network size is key—deepening ties through sustained conversations, personalized responses, and sharing of genuine support builds stronger social bonds. Actively seeking connections across different social groups nurtures bridging capital, broadening perspectives and opportunities. Platforms

61

and users alike benefit when inclusive behaviors are encouraged: ensuring diverse voices are heard, combating toxic interactions, and fostering norms of respect and empathy. Digital literacy training empowers users to engage confidently and critically, expanding the pool of contributors to social capital. Finally, integrating offline activities with online engagement grounds social capital in lived communities and sustains long-term commitment beyond fleeting digital trends.

The long-term implications of social media's impact on social capital are still unfolding. On one hand, the capacity for rapid information sharing and broad mobilization suggests enhanced community resilience in times of crisis or social change. On the other, the amplification of echo chambers, misinformation, and superficial connections risks fragmenting societal trust and weakening collective action. How these tensions play out may depend on the evolving design of platforms, the norms cultivated by users, and broader socio-political contexts. The interplay between cohesion and fragmentation in digital networks will profoundly shape not only social capital but also the fabric of society itself.

Overall, participation in social media profoundly influences the accumulation and distribution of social capital, shaping trust, reciprocity, and collective capacities. Through facilitating diverse forms of connection—from intimate support to expansive advocacy—these platforms offer fertile ground for building shared resources essential to individual and communal well-being. Yet this potential is neither automatic nor evenly realized; it requires conscious effort, equitable access, and attentive cultivation of meaningful relationships to truly enrich the social capital landscape in the digital age.

Chapter 3

Social Media and Information

This chapter investigates the transformed landscape of information in the age of social media. We begin by examining how audiences access and engage with news on digital platforms, then explore the rise of citizen journalism and its impact on traditional outlets. Building on that, we analyze the drivers and dynamics of misinformation, before presenting strategies in fact-checking and digital literacy. Next, we delve into recommendation algorithms and their role in creating information bubbles, and conclude by assessing the balance between content moderation, legal regulation, and free expression online.

3.1 News Consumption in the Digital Age

The advent of social platforms has fundamentally transformed the landscape of news consumption, shifting the power dynamics of production, distribution, and audience engagement in unprecedented ways. To grasp this transformation, it is vital to contrast the traditional broadcast model of news with today's digital media ecosystem. Historically, news operated largely on a one-way, top-down basis: professional journalists and editors curated stories, and audiences received them passively, typically through newspapers, radio, or scheduled television broadcasts. This unidirectional flow prioritized editorial gatekeeping, emphasizing accuracy, verification, and a shared news agenda.

In stark contrast, digital platforms foster an interactive, on-demand environment. News no longer arrives in fixed batches or at scheduled times; instead, it flows continuously and dynamically, responding to user input and global events almost instantaneously. This shift has not only redefined how news is accessed but also who participates in its shaping and dissemination.

Central to this evolution is the 24/7 news cycle enabled by real-time updates. Social media's immediacy facilitates live streams, instant posts, and breaking news alerts that continuously replenish the public's information buffet. Unlike the nightly news or morning papers, digital users encounter events as they unfold—whether it is a protest live-tweeted by on-the-ground witnesses or a natural disaster chronicled via successive video clips uploaded as situations develop. This immediacy can democratize information access, but it also raises challenges around verifying rapidly shared content and avoiding hasty conclusions.

Social platforms have thus become dominant news distributors, wielding tremendous influence through complex algorithms and network effects. Algorithms analyze user preferences, behaviors, and social connections to curate news feeds personalized for each individual. This tailoring means that what a person sees is rarely a neutral selection of stories but rather a prioritized mix designed to maximize engagement, keeping users scrolling and clicking. In this "attention economy," algorithmic curation can amplify certain narratives while burying others, creating a powerful if often opaque editorial force outside traditional newsroom oversight.

Alongside this, the storytelling format itself has evolved. The widespread ownership of smartphones and the rise of multimedia content—videos, gifs, audio clips, interactive graphics—have shifted news toward mobile-first reporting. Journalists and content creators now craft stories optimized for handheld screens, merging text with rich media to capture fleeting attention spans. This enriches storytelling, enabling immersive experiences, but also compels news producers to balance depth against the brevity and visual appeal demanded by online audiences.

Perhaps most striking is the role of the audience as active participants. The concept of the *prosumer*—a blend of producer and consumer—embodies this shift. Users do not merely receive news; they engage with it by commenting, sharing, adding context, or even creating their own content. Viral hashtags, citizen journalism, and crowdsourced fact-checking testify to how audiences reshape news narratives in real time. This participatory culture can enhance transparency and diversity of perspectives but also risks propagating misinformation when amateur contributions lack rigorous standards.

Engagement metrics have come to play a decisive role in shaping news visibility. Likes, shares, and comments are the currency by which stories gain traction and prominence. Algorithms interpret these signals as indicators of relevance and quality, often rewarding emotionally charged or sensational content. As a result, news items that provoke strong reactions may dominate feeds, not necessarily those with the highest journalistic integrity. This metric-driven landscape challenges traditional values of editorial judgment, incentivizing news that is clickable over news that is accurate or nuanced.

Paradoxically, the personalization that makes digital news appealing also contributes to the emergence of *filter bubbles*. Tailored feeds provide convenient but narrow selections of information aligned with users' existing beliefs and interests, potentially limiting exposure to diverse viewpoints. Over time, this can reinforce ideological silos, fragmenting public discourse and complicating constructive debate. Although algorithms aim to optimize user satisfaction, they may inadvertently deepen societal divides by confining individuals within echo chambers.

Trending topics and algorithmic curation further shape what news gains prominence. Trending lists of hashtags, stories, or videos distill the vast digital conversation into digestible highlights, steering attention toward specific events or issues. These mechanisms harness collective behavior and real-time data to elevate certain narratives, but they can also introduce volatility, with ephemeral trends overshadowing sustained coverage of complex matters. Understanding how these algorithmic "front pages" operate is crucial to decoding the pulse of contemporary news cycles.

In an environment overflowing with information, trust signals and source credibility have grown indispensable. Verified badges on social platforms, reputations of established publishers, and explicit markers of accuracy guide audiences amid a sea of content. Yet, trust is increasingly contested terrain. Misinformation, fake news, and deepfakes blur lines between authentic and fabricated stories, demanding heightened media literacy and critical consumption. Reliable news sources may use transparency, journalistic standards, and community engagement to differentiate themselves in this fragmented ecosystem.

Demographic shifts illustrate how news consumption patterns vary widely across generations and regions. Younger audiences tend to favor social media platforms such as Instagram, TikTok, and Twitter for their news intake, often valuing immediacy, visual formats, and peer endorsements. Older groups may retain preferences for traditional websites or hybrid models blending digital and legacy media. Geographic and cultural factors similarly influence which platforms dominate and how news is framed or prioritized. These differences reveal that digital news is not monolithic but a complex mosaic shaped by identity and context.

Together, these changes reveal a media environment defined by interactivity, speed, fragmentation, and personalization. Audiences today discover news through an intricate web of social platforms, algorithms, and peer networks rather than solely from traditional gatekeepers. This new terrain offers unparalleled opportunities for engagement and diversity but also poses significant challenges related to reliability, equity, and democratic discourse. Navigating the digital news age requires both an appreciation of these dynamics and a critical eye toward how technology reshapes what we see, share, and believe.

3.2 Citizen Journalism

In a media landscape long dominated by newspapers, television, and professional correspondents, citizen journalism has emerged as a transformative force. At its core, citizen journalism refers to ordinary individuals—those without formal training or affiliation to established news organizations—using digital tools to report and share news events. Unlike professional reporters, who operate under editorial guidelines and often possess journalistic training, citizen journalists act independently, bringing immediacy, personal experience, and unfiltered perspectives to public discourse.

The genesis of citizen journalism can be traced back to the early internet era, where personal blogs and grass-roots forums became incubators for informal reporting. In the late 1990s and early 2000s, platforms such as Live-Journal and independent weblogs allowed individuals to document local happenings or offer alternative takes on mainstream news. These digital spaces were often experimental and fragmented but crucially demonstrated the hunger for diverse voices outside professional gate-keeping. Early forums like Usenet and community bulletin boards also provided venues for rapid exchange of information, sowing seeds for participatory news sharing.

A key catalyst for citizen journalism has been the rapid evolution of enabling technologies. Smartphones equipped with high-quality cameras, combined with always-on internet connectivity, have turned nearly everyone into a potential reporter. Live-streaming apps like Periscope, Facebook Live, and now TikTok allow witnesses to broadcast unfolding events in real time, while social media platforms provide immediate avenues for distribution. This technological empowerment dismantles previous barriers to entry, allowing users to capture and share moments with unprecedented speed and reach.

Speed is, in fact, one of citizen journalism's distinct advantages. Eyewitnesses with smartphones often break news faster than traditional media, especially in fast-moving or remote stories. Consider the instant circulation of video footage from events such as natural disasters, protests, or accidents, often arriving on social media timelines minutes before official press reports. This immediacy is a double-edged sword—while it delivers a valuable first look, it also challenges conventional newsrooms accustomed to verification and editorial processes before publication.

Beyond speed, citizen journalism enhances diversity and representation within the media ecosystem. Traditional outlets can struggle to cover marginalized communities or sensitive issues comprehensively, either due to resource limitations or editorial biases. Citizen journalists, embedded within particular communities or contexts, bring unique vantage points especially relevant to local or under-reported stories. By amplifying voices from varied socio-economic, ethnic, and cultural backgrounds, citizen journalism contributes to a richer, more pluralistic public conversation.

However, along with its many strengths, citizen journalism faces profound challenges in verification and accuracy. The absence of formal training and editorial oversight means that unverified rumors, misinterpretations, or manipulated content can spread rapidly. Misleading images and videos can sow confusion or inflame tensions, as witnessed during moments of political unrest or public health crises. Strategies for corroboration often rely on cross-checking multiple independent sources, geolocation tools to authenticate imagery, and crowdsourced fact-checking initiatives. News organizations increasingly deploy digital forensics teams to assess user-generated material before amplifying it.

Ethical and legal considerations loom large over the practice of citizen journalism. Privacy concerns surface when individuals capture footage of others without consent, especially in sensitive or vulnerable situations. Consent becomes particularly fraught during emergencies or protests, where identities revealed in user content may attract retaliation. Moreover, questions of liability arise—when should citizen-generated content be considered defamatory, or when must its publishers assume responsibility for harm caused by dissemination? Navigating this terrain requires a balance between freedom of expression and protection of individual rights, often with little clear precedent.

Despite these challenges, collaboration between citizen journalists and traditional media outlets has grown into a dynamic partnership. Professional newsrooms increasingly source eyewitness materials as supplements or leads for their coverage, recognizing the firsthand value of user-generated content. Journalists apply their editorial judgment to verify and contextualize these inputs, blending the immediacy of citizen reportage with the rigor and perspective of institutional journalism. This synthesis enriches news narratives while helping guard against misinformation.

Citizen journalism has had profound impacts on crisis and human-rights reporting worldwide. Notable examples include videos from the Arab Spring uprisings, where citizens' smartphones recorded and disseminated scenes of demonstrations and state repression, galvanizing international interest and support. Similarly, footage captured by bystanders during police violence or humanitarian disasters has pressured authorities and shaped public opinion in ways traditional media could not have achieved alone. Such instances illustrate citizen journalism's potential as a tool for accountability and social justice.

Taken together, the rise of citizen journalism reshapes the contemporary media landscape in complex ways. On one hand, it democratizes information, injecting immediacy, plurality, and grassroots authenticity into news flows. On the other, it raises inevitable questions about credibility, ethics, and the evolving roles of professional journalists. Far from displacing traditional media, citizen journalism often acts as both a supplement and a challenge, urging the entire ecosystem to rethink how stories are sourced, verified, and told in the digital age.

3.3 The Spread of Misinformation

Misinformation, disinformation, and malinformation form a triad of misleading content that disrupts the delicate fabric of online discourse. Although often used interchangeably, these terms carry distinct nuances with significant implications. *Misinformation* refers to false or inaccurate information shared without malicious intent—someone might unknowingly spread a distorted news story or mistaken health advice. In contrast, *disinformation* is deliberately fabricated or manipulated content designed to deceive, often employed strategically to sway public opinion or obscure the truth. *Malinformation* differs again; it involves the use of genuine information—sometimes private or sensitive—with the intent to cause harm, such as leaking personal data to disgrace individuals or communities. This taxonomy helps unravel the complex motivations behind why false and harmful content arises and proliferates online, framing the challenges that follow.

The drivers fueling the spread of misinformation are as varied as human ambition itself. At one level, profit motives dominate: sensational headlines and emotionally charged stories attract clicks and shares, translating into advertising revenue for websites and platforms. Clickbait thrives on human curiosity and outrage, incentiviz-ing content producers to prioritize engagement over ac-curacy. Politics, too, is a powerful accelerant. Political actors and interest groups often harness misinformation to undermine opponents, galvanize supporters, or sup-press dissent, crafting narratives that simplify complex realities into easily digestible slogans. Social incentives are equally potent; in an era where likes and retweets equate to social capital, individuals may unwittingly be-come vectors of falsehoods, seeking affirmation within their communities.

The architecture of online networks compounds these effects by creating echo chambers—digital environments where individuals predominantly encounter opinions that mirror their own. Algorithms designed to maximize engagement often encourage homophily, clustering people around shared beliefs and values. Within these insulated communities, misinformation finds fertile ground; unverified claims rarely face rigorous scrutiny, while skepticism is discouraged or viewed as disloyalty. This homogeneity amplifies the perceived legitimacy of false narratives, transforming fringe ideas into accepted truths by sheer repetition. The network's structure thus isolates users from corrective information, reinforcing biases and deepening divides.

Psychology plays a pivotal role in shaping how misinformation embeds itself within minds and spreads between users. Confirmation bias leads individuals to favor information that aligns with pre-existing beliefs while ignoring contradictory evidence. This selective exposure reduces cognitive dissonance and maintains a coherent worldview, even when it rests on shaky foundations. Emotional arousal—particularly fear, anger, or moral outrage—heightens the likelihood of sharing, as emotionally charged content elicits stronger reactions and more immediate impulses to disseminate. Cognitive shortcuts, or heuristics, simplify complex information, but these mental rules of thumb can lead to misjudgments about credibility. Together, these psychological tendencies accelerate the viral spread of falsehoods, as rational evaluation of content often gives way to gut reactions and social identity considerations.

The modern battleground for information is further complicated by automated bots and coordinated campaigns that manipulate public discourse. Bots—programmed accounts that can imitate real users—are deployed at scale to amplify specific messages, artificially inflating popularity and creating the illusion of consensus. These entities can retweet, comment, and post content relentlessly, overwhelming human attempts to interject accurate information. Coordinated campaigns may synchronize hundreds or thousands of such accounts, enabling rapid dissemination of disinformation with precision and persistence previously unthinkable. They can target particular demographics, flood hashtags, or drown out dissenting voices, distorting the genuine dynamics of online conversation.

Underlying these phenomena are striking differences in how false and accurate information propagate. Studies have shown that misinformation often spreads faster, farther, and more broadly than verified news. False news stories tend to evoke stronger emotional responses, crucial for virality, and are often novel or surprising, capturing attention in ways mundane factual reports cannot. Moreover, falsehoods may persist longer in the collective memory; corrections and fact-checks frequently fail to travel as swiftly or gain equivalent traction. This asymmetry means that even with robust editorial efforts and technological interventions, misinformation maintains a stubborn foothold, continuously resurfacing in conversations and shaping perceptions.

Historical snapshots reveal the tangible impact of misinformation during critical moments. The 2016 U.S. presidential election famously illustrated how false rumors and fabricated news stories circulated widely across social media, sowing confusion and distrust. Conspiracies about voter fraud, manipulated poll results, and candidate scandals were widely shared, affecting public confidence in the electoral process. Similarly, public health crises—like the Ebola outbreak or the COVID-19 pandemic—have been marred by hoaxes and misleading claims about cures, transmission, or vaccines. These false narratives not only hindered effective responses but sometimes triggered harmful behaviors, such as avoiding treatment or rejecting life-saving vaccines, with real-world consequences for morbidity and mortality.

The societal repercussions of misinformation extend beyond momentary confusion; they erode trust in institutions, fray social cohesion, and fuel polarization. When citizens doubt the integrity of news outlets, governments, or scientific authorities, the foundation for collective decision-making weakens. Political polarization deepens as communities retreat further into ideological enclaves, less willing to engage with opposing views or factual evidence. This fragmentation impairs democratic deliberation, fostering cynicism and disengagement. On a practical level, misinformation influences behaviors—ranging from voting patterns to health choices—sometimes placing lives and livelihoods at risk. In sum, the ripple effects of false content permeate social, political, and individual spheres, reshaping reality itself.

The dynamics of misinformation reflect a complex interplay of incentives, network effects, cognitive biases, and technological tools. The resilience of false content online owes much to its emotional appeal, rapid diffusion through echo chambers, and amplification by automated actors. Overcoming these challenges requires a nuanced understanding of how and why misinformation thrives, coupled with multifaceted strategies spanning education, platform governance, and technological innovation. Recognizing the forces that propel falsehoods is the first step toward cultivating a digital environment where truth has a fighting chance.

3.4 Fact-Checking and Digital Literacy

Navigating today's vast digital ecosystem demands more than casual scrolling; it requires a refined set of skills often grouped under the umbrella of digital and news literacy. At its core, digital literacy is the competency to locate, evaluate, and interpret information online with a critical eye, while news literacy hones in on discerning fact from fiction in media messages. Together, they equip individuals to sift fact from fabrication in a landscape where misinformation can travel faster than truth.

A fundamental part of these competencies is understanding that not all information encountered online is created equal. Finding a claim is simple; discerning its reliability involves questioning the source's credibility, examining the evidence provided, and evaluating the broader context. These steps form the basis of what educators often call critical and lateral reading. Critical reading urges the reader to assess a single source's trustworthiness, scrutinizing authorship, expertise, and potential biases. Lateral reading, on the other hand, entails stepping outside the initial source and consulting a variety of references—other news outlets, specialized databases, or official fact-checkers—to cross-check claims and expose inconsistencies or corroborations. This lateral movement across sources combats echo chambers and encourages more nuanced understanding.

For example, encountering a viral image purportedly showing a dramatic event might tempt a quick share. But employing practical verification methods can unveil deception. Reverse-image search tools, such as Google Images or TinEye, allow a user to upload the picture and see where else it appears online—sometimes revealing an original context entirely different from that claimed. Metadata inspection, which examines embedded details like timestamps, geolocation, or device information, can offer clues about authenticity or reveal manipulation. Cross-referencing timestamps and reported events with trusted news timelines further sharpens accuracy. These methods empower individuals to piece together the true narrative behind a digital artifact.

Beyond individual effort, professional fact-checking organizations provide an essential backstop against misinformation. Groups like FactCheck.org, PolitiFact, and Snopes rely on systematic workflows to verify claims circulating in public discourse. Their process typically unfolds in stages:

- Identifying suspicious assertions,

- Gathering relevant evidence through research and expert consultation,

- Assessing the veracity of the claim, and

- Publishing clear, accessible verdicts—often with source citations and contextual explanation.

Crucially, these organizations correct errors transparently, contributing to public trust in their work and modeling intellectual humility in a contested information environment.

Recognizing the need to guide users in real-time, digital platforms increasingly deploy labels and informational cues embedded directly in news feeds and social media posts. Warning banners might flag content disputed by fact-checkers; context panels can provide background on trending topics or the credibility of the publisher; and tags may clarify if a piece is satire or sponsored content. These cues serve as gentle nudges to slow down and reflect before accepting or sharing information. While not foolproof—often sparking debates about censorship or bias—they represent a significant evolution in the architecture of information consumption.

Complementing professional fact-checkers, crowd-sourced models harness the wisdom of communities to evaluate content. Platforms like Wikipedia thrive on peer review and collective moderation, where volunteers—often experts or enthusiasts in specific fields—engage in continuous scrutiny and revision. Social media experiments with community flagging and deliberative feedback loops attempt to leverage network effects for fact-checking. Although these approaches face challenges of scale and potential groupthink, they illustrate the power and limits of decentralized verification in an era of overwhelming information volume.

In parallel with technical tools and community efforts, education remains an indispensable pillar to cultivate critical media skills from an early age. Many schools and universities now integrate digital literacy into their curricula, blending lessons on source evaluation, online ethics, and the mechanics of misinformation. Online courses, webinars, and public awareness campaigns expand access beyond formal education, democratizing knowledge about information verification techniques. These initiatives aim to build not only competence but also a healthy skepticism—an attitude that questions rather than instantly trusts, without lapsing into cynicism.

Despite these layered efforts, fact-checking faces significant challenges related to scalability and user motivation. The sheer speed and volume of digital content mean that even the most dedicated organizations can verify only a fraction of circulating claims, often reacting after misinformation has already spread widely. Additionally, cognitive biases and social identities influence how individuals process corrections; some may resist or dismiss fact-checks if they conflict with deeply held beliefs. Thus, the battlefield is not solely informational but also psychological and cultural, demanding multifaceted strategies beyond mere fact verification.

This complexity underscores the importance of building long-term resilience against misinformation through habits and institutional design. Individuals benefit from cultivating routines: pausing before sharing, consulting diverse news sources, and nurturing curiosity rather than passive consumption. At an institutional level, platforms can design interfaces that promote reflection and make credible information more visible and attractive, while educators and policymakers can support ongoing literacy initiatives. Together, these efforts create a more informed public less vulnerable to manipulation and more equipped to uphold democratic discourse.

Bringing these elements into harmony reveals a suite of effective strategies for navigating the misinformation landscape. Employing critical and lateral reading techniques encourages scrutiny beyond first impressions. Utilizing verification tools like reverse-image search and metadata inspection grounds understanding in evidence. Trusting reputable fact-checking organizations, while recognizing their limits, offers guidance in complex debates. Paying heed to platform labels sharpens awareness of context and credibility. Engaging in crowdsourced review can enhance community vigilance. Supporting education ensures these skills diffuse broadly and deepen over time. Finally, acknowledging challenges in motivation and scalability reminds us that digital literacy is a continual journey rather than a single skill to acquire.

Together, these approaches transform the daunting flood of digital content into a navigable stream, enabling individuals not just to survive but thrive as critical consumers in a media-saturated world.

3.5 Algorithms and Information Bubbles

At the heart of today's digital experience lie recommendation algorithms—complex yet often invisible engines that tailor the vast ocean of online content into a manageable stream personalized for each user. These algorithms power everything from streaming platforms suggesting the next binge-worthy series to social media feeds sequencing posts designed to catch and hold our attention. While these personalization engines offer convenience and engagement, they also shape the diversity and quality of information we encounter, subtly steering what we see and hear. To grasp their impact, it is crucial to understand how these algorithms function, the inputs they rely on, and the social consequences that follow.

Recommendation algorithms typically fall into three broad categories: collaborative filtering, content-based filtering, and hybrid models. Collaborative filtering operates by identifying patterns in the behavior of many users to recommend items favored by those with similar tastes. For example, if two users enjoy many of the same movies, a collaborative filtering system might suggest the films liked by one user to the other. Content-based filtering, on the other hand, recommends items similar in attributes to what a user has previously engaged with, such as suggesting articles that share themes or keywords with those already read. Hybrid models combine these approaches to balance personalization and serendipity, aiming to mitigate the weaknesses of each method when used alone. The nuanced interplay of these techniques allows platforms to produce recommendations that feel both relevant and fresh, though the underlying logic is a careful dance between predicting preferences and encouraging discovery.

Data inputs and user signals provide the raw material for these algorithms. Everything from clicks, likes, and shares to watch time and scrolling behavior feeds into the system's understanding of what captivates an individual. Watch time is particularly telling; spending minutes engrossed in a video signals stronger interest than a quick click. Engagement metrics, such as comments or content sharing, add another layer of insight, suggesting deeper involvement. Together, these signals help algorithms prioritize certain content, optimizing for what is predicted to maximize user interaction. Yet, this focus on engagement carries subtle implications for the kinds of information that surface, often privileging emotionally charged, sensational, or easily digestible content over nuanced or challenging perspectives.

The personalization that algorithms provide carries with it the risk of filter bubbles and echo chambers—concepts that have gained traction in discussions about the social impact of digital media. A filter bubble forms when the automated curation process isolates users within a narrow range of content, essentially surrounding them with information that reinforces their existing beliefs and interests. An echo chamber extends the metaphor to social dynamics, where a user's social network amplifies similar viewpoints, limiting exposure to dissenting opinions. Both phenomena can diminish cognitive diversity, fostering selective attention and potentially entrenching biases. While tailored content feels personalized and convenient, it may inadvertently constrict intellectual horizons, reducing encounters with alternative worldviews essential for balanced understanding.

These consequences have sparked considerable research linking algorithmic curation to growing social and political polarization. Studies have found that users on platforms heavily reliant on recommendation engines are more likely to engage with ideologically homogenous content, sometimes even drifting toward more extreme viewpoints over time. The feedback loop created by reinforcing preferences can harden divides, making social discourse more fragmented and antagonistic. Platforms like YouTube, Facebook, and Twitter have been scrutinized for their roles in shaping public opinion, with some evidence showing that the design of their recommendation systems can inadvertently promote divisive or misleading content. The complexity of this issue stems partly from the challenge of balancing personalization—with its benefits of engagement and relevance—and the need to foster a healthy informational ecosystem that supports exposure to diverse voices.

Calls for algorithmic transparency and explainability have responded to these concerns, emphasizing the need for platforms to demystify how recommendations are generated. Transparency here means going beyond abstract statements, moving toward public reporting of algorithm design principles, data usage, and content moderation policies. Explainability seeks to provide users with understandable, user-facing insights into why specific recommendations appear—such as labels indicating "Recommended because you watched..." or options to adjust preferences. Such initiatives aim to empower users, enabling greater awareness and control over their digital environments. However, the technical complexity and proprietary nature of recommendation engines pose significant challenges, and full transparency risks enabling manipulation or gaming of the system, adding tension to this evolving debate.

To counteract the narrowing effects of personalization, platforms and researchers have explored various interventions designed to diversify the content users encounter. One approach involves injecting random or less predictable recommendations into feeds, intentionally disrupting the feedback loop. Cross-ideological prompts encourage users to engage with viewpoints outside their comfort zones, sometimes through curated sets of contrasting perspectives. Additionally, user controls that allow individuals to customize the breadth and types of content they receive provide a more participatory form of diversification. These strategies, while promising, must tread carefully between nudging users toward edgier or more balanced content and respecting autonomy and preference, an intricate balance that highlights the role of design choices in shaping online experiences.

Underlying this complex landscape is a fundamental design trade-off between maximizing engagement and promoting informational health. Engagement-driven algorithms prioritize metrics like clicks, watch time, and shares, often rewarding content that provokes strong emotional reactions or confirms existing biases. However, such content may not always align with the broader societal goal of fostering an informed and open-minded citizenry. Informational health, in this context, refers to the quality, diversity, and credibility of the content audiences receive, supporting critical reflection and exposure to varied viewpoints. Balancing these competing incentives requires both technological innovation and a commitment to ethical design principles, reckoning with the fact that what is most captivating is not always what is most beneficial.

Algorithm Type	Strengths	Weaknesses
Collaborative Filtering	Leverages collective user behavior; uncovers novel recommendations outside user's history	Suffers from cold-start problem (new users/items); may reinforce popular trends, reducing diversity
Content-Based Filtering	Tailors recommendations based on user's own history; effective for niche preferences	Limited serendipity; can trap users in narrow interest profiles
Hybrid Models	Combines the strengths of both to improve accuracy and diversity	Increased complexity; harder to interpret and debug

Table 3.1: Comparison of Recommendation Algorithm Types

Looking ahead, emerging personalization techniques promise refinements that could better balance user agency, privacy, and informational richness. Federated learning, for instance, enables algorithms to train on decentralized user data stored locally on devices, reducing privacy risks while maintaining personalization. This approach also opens possibilities for greater transparency and user involvement in shaping recommendation logic. Another frontier is the development of user-configurable filters and adjustable algorithmic parameters, allowing users to choose the degree of personalization or diversity they prefer. Such innovations reflect a shift from opaque, one-size-fits-all systems toward more participatory and adaptable models, potentially mitigating the isolating effects of current algorithms.

Ultimately, personalization engines embody a paradox: they simultaneously serve as indispensable tools for managing vast content landscapes and as mechanisms capable of narrowing informational horizons. Their design and deployment influence not just what information reaches users, but how societies negotiate knowledge, culture, and consensus. Understanding this dual role is vital for anyone navigating the digital world, highlighting the importance of mindful algorithmic design, informed choice, and ongoing public dialogue about the invisible intermediaries shaping the information bubbles we inhabit.

3.6 Censorship and Freedom of Expression

The digital realm has become a sprawling public square where ideas, opinions, and information collide, intertwine, and sometimes clash. Central to this dynamic space are two competing imperatives: the desire to safeguard free expression, a cornerstone of democratic societies, and the need to moderate content that may cause harm, spread misinformation, or incite violence. This ongoing balancing act takes shape through complex interactions among users, platforms, and legal authorities, exposing persistent tensions over who controls speech online, to what extent, and under what principles.

At its core, *censorship* refers to the suppression, restriction, or removal of speech, ideas, or information. Online, this can manifest as the deletion of posts, shadow banning of users, or complete account suspensions. It often provokes alarm due to fears over authoritarian overreach or stifling of dissent. Conversely, *freedom of expression* embodies the right to seek, receive, and impart information—values enshrined in international declarations such as Article 19 of the Universal Declaration of Human Rights. In the digital age, these rights extend to myriad platforms functioning as modern agoras, where governance must grapple not only with speech itself but also with unprecedented scale and speed.

Platforms have stepped into the breach as de facto arbiters, crafting *content policies* designed to define acceptable speech within their ecosystems. These *community standards* set boundaries—prohibiting hate speech, harassment, sexually explicit content, or misinformation, among others—while striving to uphold open discourse. Enforcement is facilitated by a growing arsenal of *moderation tools*, from automated algorithms scanning billions of posts daily to human reviewers assessing flagged content. Transparency has emerged as a key accountability mechanism, with many companies publishing *transparency reports* revealing takedown statistics, policy enforcement trends, and appeals outcomes, allowing public scrutiny of their gatekeeping role.

Yet, moderation is rarely straightforward or consistent. Platforms wrestle with *policy gaps* arising from ambiguous definitions or cross-cultural content sensitivities. Limited resources and the sheer volume of user activity lead to *enforcement trade-offs*: automated systems can overreach, removing benign content, while human moderators face burnout and error. The variance in policies across platforms and regions fuels user confusion and uneven protections, sometimes amplifying misinformation or allowing harmful content to persist.

Beyond private governance, governments weigh in through *statutory regulation*—laws that set mandatory requirements for content removal or liability for hosting. These legal frameworks often conflict or overlap with voluntary platform moderation, creating a patchwork of authority. In the United States, Section 230 of the Communications Decency Act provides a foundational protection, shielding platforms from liability for user-generated content while allowing discretion in moderation. Meanwhile, the European Union's General Data Protection Regulation (GDPR) focuses on privacy rights but indirectly shapes content governance through data-handling rules. The Digital Millennium Copyright Act (DMCA) exemplifies targeted regulation, authorizing *notice-and-takedown* procedures to combat copyright infringement online.

Notice-and-takedown processes grant content owners a mechanism to request removal of infringing material, which platforms must act upon promptly to retain legal safe harbor protections. However, these procedures have stirred debate over *user recourse*, as wrongful takedowns can suppress lawful speech with limited immediate remedy. Appeals systems and content reinstatement policies have emerged as crucial checks, though their efficacy varies widely.

Amid evolving policy landscapes, users often face *self-censorship*, tempering or silencing their own expression out of uncertainty or fear of surveillance and retaliation. This *chilling effect* reflects how opaque moderation guidelines and government monitoring can inadvertently deter participation in public discourse, potentially narrowing the diversity of voices heard online. The tension between privacy and transparency becomes particularly pronounced where platforms cooperate extensively with state authorities or where misinformation concerns prompt aggressive content filtering.

Global perspectives reveal starkly different moderation ecosystems shaped by political regimes and cultural norms. Democracies may emphasize free expression tempered by legal protections, while authoritarian states often impose stringent censorship to maintain control. For example, platforms operating in China contend with government-mandated content restrictions that contrast sharply with the more open, though still contested, environments of North America and Europe. These *international case studies* illustrate how moderation is entangled not just with technology, but with ideology and power.

The roles of *anonymity and encryption* further complicate this landscape. Anonymity can empower marginalized voices and whistleblowers, safeguarding expression where identifiable speech risks persecution. Encryption guarantees privacy and security, often making content beyond the reach of moderation tools. Yet, these same features can hinder efforts to combat harmful or illegal content, illustrating that privacy protections and content control can come into conflict.

Censorship and moderation also have profound implications for *journalism and activism.* Digital platforms serve as critical venues for reporting, mobilizing social movements, and amplifying underrepresented narratives. Content removals—whether driven by policy or government pressure—can disrupt these functions, chilling investigative journalism or silencing protest voices. Conversely, unchecked misinformation or hate speech can erode trust in media and democracy, underscoring the double-edged nature of content governance.

Finding a sustainable *balance* requires thoughtful policy design and multi-stakeholder collaboration. Recommended principles include:

- Prioritizing transparency around moderation criteria and decisions,

- Ensuring user participation in appeal mechanisms,

- Contextualizing harmful content rather than resorting to blanket removal,

- Fostering media literacy among users.

Regulators and platforms alike must appreciate the nuance—inclusiveness, proportionality, and respect for fundamental rights—needed to mediate between protecting users from harm and preserving a vibrant, open exchange of ideas.

The persistent *dynamics of expression and control* online reflect broader societal struggles over power, identity, and community. Digital spaces amplify the stakes and scale of these conflicts but also present novel opportunities for negotiation and innovation. Rather than envision censorship and freedom of expression as binary antagonists, understanding their interplay can illuminate pathways toward more equitable, resilient digital public spheres.

Chapter 4

Psychological Effects of Social Media

This chapter examines how social media interactions shape our mental processes and emotional well-being. We begin by unpacking the feedback mechanisms—likes, comments, and reactions—that drive validation and self-esteem. We then explore compulsive usage patterns born from addictive design features, before confronting the harms of online harassment. Next, we analyze the impact of social comparison on self-image, and offer strategies for mindful engagement. Finally, we highlight resources and communities that support mental health in the digital era.

4.1 The Psychology of Likes and Validation

Social feedback, the currency of the digital age, manifests in subtle yet powerful forms: likes, comments, shares, and reactions. Each represents a distinct way people acknowledge, endorse, or engage with our self-expression online. A *like* is the simplest nod of approval, often a quick tap that signals "I see you." Comments offer more personalized interaction, a written response that can range from praise to critique. Shares expand the audience by passing content along, implicitly vouching for its value. Finally, reactions—those colorful emoji-like buttons—allow nuanced emotional responses, from laughter to sympathy. Together, these feedback mechanisms form a complex ecosystem where social affirmation is both quantified and experienced.

At the core of this ecosystem lies the brain's neurobiological reward system, particularly the dopamine pathways. Dopamine, often described as the brain's pleasure chemical, is released not only in response to tangible rewards like food or money but also social rewards. When a person receives a like or positive comment, neurons in areas such as the ventral striatum and nucleus accumbens activate, signaling a hit of reward. This neural reaction reinforces the behavior that led to the social approval, encouraging further interaction and sharing. What makes social feedback uniquely compelling is that it ties our social standing directly to these biological circuits, making digital affirmations feel momentarily as vital as in-person praise and acceptance.

The potency of social feedback is enhanced by the unpredictable nature of its delivery, a phenomenon known as variable-ratio reinforcement. Unlike fixed schedules where rewards appear predictably, variable schedules dispense feedback at irregular intervals and quantities. In the context of social media, users rarely know when the next wave of likes or comments will arrive. This uncertainty fosters anticipation and keeps users checking their feeds compulsively, much like the allure of gambling machines. Because the brain cannot predict exactly when the next dopamine release will occur, the behavior—posting, refreshing, scrolling—strengthens, driven by the hope of a social reward that might come at any moment.

Timing plays a crucial role in reinforcing this cycle. Instant gratification, delivered through real-time notifications, maximizes the impact of feedback. A ping, vibration, or sound signals an immediate social reward, drawing attention sharply and elevating mood. These timely alerts create micro-moments of joy or social connection that can punctuate the day. However, they can also fragment focus, drawing users repeatedly back into screens. The rapid cycle between action and feedback heightens engagement, embedding social validation into daily rhythms and making the quest for approval both urgent and habitual.

An important dimension shaping psychological outcomes is the public or private nature of feedback. Public metrics—visible like counts, share tallies, and comment threads—offer a transparent, comparative measure of social approval. Because these numbers are often displayed prominently, they not only inform the individual's sense of worth but can also influence how others perceive them. In contrast, private feedback, such as direct messages or hidden reactions, carries a different emotional weight: more intimate, less performative, and sometimes more meaningful for personal relationships. Public endorsements can lead to social competition or pressure, while private affirmations can nurture closeness without the gaze of the crowd.

This interplay between external approval and self-worth reveals a profound psychological phenomenon: the fusion of validation with personal identity. When social feedback becomes a primary gauge of one's value, it can shape self-esteem and self-concept in powerful ways. A flood of likes might temporarily lift feelings of competence and belonging, whereas sparse or negative responses may trigger doubt or diminished confidence. Over time, the digital tally of affirmation can feel like a personal scoreboard, making the individual's sense of self contingent upon external applause. This alignment turns social platforms into arenas where identity is performed, negotiated, and measured through feedback loops.

Such external reliance introduces anxiety around performance, particularly for content creators and active social media participants. The fear of low engagement—few likes, absent comments, or scarce shares—can provoke feelings of rejection and failure. For creators, whose digital output is intertwined with personal expression, this anxiety may lead to second-guessing, self-censorship, or over-curation of posts to appease anticipated audiences. The invisible yet pervasive pressure to maintain or grow social approval impacts not only creativity but also emotional well-being, highlighting the delicate balance between expression and external judgment.

Platform designers are keenly aware of these psychological dynamics and engineer interfaces to maximize user engagement by amplifying reward signals. Algorithms prioritize content likely to garner reactions, while user interfaces employ variable reinforcement principles to keep attention captured. Features like badges, streak counts, and visible like counters tap into competitive and reward-driven instincts. Notifications are timed and tailored to prompt return visits, creating a cycle where technology and psychology collaborate to foster deeper, often compulsive, involvement. These feedback loops are not accidental; they harness our brain's innate response patterns to social stimuli, optimizing the platform's appeal and stickiness.

The types of feedback offered by platforms have grown more diverse and nuanced, reflecting evolving understandings of social emotion and communication. Beyond simple likes, options such as laughing emojis, heart reactions, or sad faces allow users to express complex responses that shape emotional tone and interpersonal dynamics. Interactive tools like polls or story replies invite active participation and can reinforce community connections. This variety enables more subtle and personalized social signaling, influencing how individuals interpret feedback and how they themselves engage. The emotional palette expands, fostering richer, sometimes more authentic, exchanges than a simple thumbs-up.

Taken together, these dynamics illustrate how social feedback shapes behavior, mood, and self-perception in profound ways. The quest for likes and validation is more than a trivial pastime—it taps into ancient psychological mechanisms underlying social bonding and self-esteem. The digital environment magnifies these effects by quantifying approval, enabling instant gratification, and fostering complex social comparisons. As users engage with these feedback systems, they navigate a powerful terrain where biology, technology, and identity intersect, with consequences that reach far beyond the screen.

4.2 Addiction and Overuse

The term *digital addiction* captures a genuine phenomenon: the compulsive, often uncontrollable
engagement with social media platforms that disrupts
daily life. Defining this addiction hinges less on moral
judgment and more on observable patterns—persistent
use despite negative consequences, an inability to
reduce or stop engagement, and withdrawal symptoms
when offline. Unlike stepping into a library or watching
television, social media is engineered to hook attention
through a continuous flow of varied, personalized
content. When individuals find themselves unable to
resist returning to these platforms despite harm to their

well-being, their usage crosses from healthy interaction into problematic overuse.

Central to this dynamic are the design features embedded within social media platforms that foster engagement by exploiting human psychology. Infinite scroll, for example, removes natural stopping cues, delivering a seamless stream of content that blurs the boundary between voluntary use and compulsion. Instead of discrete pages or chapters, users are presented with an endless feed that tempts them to linger longer— an effect amplified by autoplay mechanisms that automatically play videos or stories without requiring a click. Persistent notifications serve as digital taps on the shoulder, demanding attention at unpredictable intervals. These features together craft a user experience that subtly erodes autonomy, making it difficult to disengage or set limits.

The psychological underpinning of such compulsive use can be understood through the *craving–withdrawal cycle*. Anticipating notifications or new content triggers a craving state—akin to hunger—that motivates repeated checking of devices. When these anticipated updates fail to appear, or when access is interrupted, users often experience distress or irritation, signaling a mild withdrawal. This cycle mirrors classical addiction models where the brain's reward system, conditioned by intermittent reinforcement, intensifies the desire for the next dopamine hit. Over time, what began as curiosity or casual browsing can morph into a habitual, sometimes automatic behavior pattern, resistant to conscious control.

Fueling this cycle is the pervasive anxiety known as the *fear of missing out* (FOMO). The modern social media landscape incessantly broadcasts events, opinions, and conversations, suggesting that meaningful experiences unfold continuously elsewhere. This perceived social scarcity compels individuals to check their feeds obsessively, lest they fall behind or be excluded from group knowledge and social currency. FOMO not only sustains the craving to stay connected but amplifies social comparison and dissatisfaction, creating a fertile ground for emotional distress.

Such compulsive engagement reshapes daily routines through *usage patterns and time displacement*. Time once allocated to focused work, restful sleep, or face-to-face interactions is frequently siphoned off by social media. This not only impairs productivity but interrupts the restorative cycles crucial to mental and physical health. The allure of brief digital escapes often fragments what should be extended periods of concentration or relaxation, producing a paradox where users feel simultaneously busy and unproductive.

This fragmentation extends to cognitive functioning, as *attention fragmentation* ensues. Multitasking—juggling social media notifications with other tasks—undermines sustained focus and increases mental fatigue. Rather than enhancing efficiency, this constant switching exacts a toll on working memory and executive function. Studies demonstrate that frequent interruptions from digital media reduce the brain's capacity to filter distractions and deepen engagement, leading to shallower processing and diminished creativity.

A particularly insidious consequence of excessive social media use is its impact on *sleep and well-being*. Engagement peaks typically coincide with evening hours, delaying bedtime and reducing overall sleep duration. The blue light emitted by screens further disrupts circadian rhythms by suppressing melatonin production. Poor sleep is tightly linked to impairments in mood regulation, cognitive function, and overall health, creating a vicious cycle where fatigue fuels more screen time as a means of stimulation or escape.

Paradoxically, the *social isolation* often feared as a consequence of digital withdrawal also emerges from heavy online use. Though platforms promise connection, extended virtual engagement can erode real-world relationships, substituting the depth of face-to-face interaction with superficial digital exchanges. This replacement reduces opportunities for meaningful bonding and can exacerbate feelings of loneliness. Ironically, those most anxious about missing out may find themselves more socially isolated in tangible terms, trapped in a feedback loop of seeking connection through increasingly shallow digital contacts.

Recognizing when usage has tipped into addiction is crucial. Behavioral signs include persistent preoccupation with social media, unsuccessful attempts to cut back, increased tolerance (needing more time to feel satisfied), withdrawal symptoms such as irritability or restlessness when offline, and neglect of responsibilities or personal interests. These indicators often co-occur with emotional distress, ranging from anxiety to depression, painting a picture of digital engagement as a compulsive behavior with tangible costs.

Taken together, the consequences of addiction and overuse reveal a multifaceted erosion of cognitive, social, and emotional well-being. Cognitively, constant exposure to fragmented content undermines attention and depth of thought. Socially, the promise of connection often dissolves into isolation and weakened interpersonal bonds. Emotionally, the compulsive cycle heightens anxiety, fuels dissatisfaction, and disrupts the restorative power of sleep. While digital media remain powerful tools for communication and information, their design and usage patterns demand greater awareness to avoid the pitfalls of addiction and to reclaim balanced, intentional engagement with the digital world.

4.3 Online Harassment and Bullying

The digital age has transformed how we communicate, but it has also ushered in new ways for hostility to manifest. Online harassment—an umbrella term for hostile behaviors directed at individuals or groups through digital platforms—has become an alarming social problem. Understanding its forms, effects, and responses demands a nuanced look at what constitutes harassment in these virtual spaces.

At its core, online harassment includes a range of behaviors that intentionally cause distress or harm to others. *Trolling*, for example, involves deliberately provoking or upsetting individuals to elicit emotional reactions or disrupt conversations. Unlike benign disagreements, trolling is characterized by persistent antagonism and often thrives on anonymity. *Cyberbullying* is a more targeted form of harassment, typically involving repeated and hostile actions aimed at a particular victim, often manifesting among younger users but by no means limited to them. *Doxxing* involves the malicious release of private or identifying information online, exposing victims to potential offline dangers as well. *Hate speech*, meanwhile, uses derogatory language based on race, gender, religion, sexual orientation, or other identities to demean or incite hostility against marginalized groups. These terms are distinct but sometimes overlap, creating a complex ecosystem of abuse across social networks, forums, and comment sections.

One key factor amplifying these behaviors is the veil of *anonymity* and the psychological phenomenon known as the *online disinhibition effect*. When people interact behind usernames or without face-to-face contact, their sense of accountability diminishes. Social restraints that typically prevent overt aggression in real life relax, allowing individuals to express hostility with fewer immediate consequences. This perceived freedom can escalate even minor disagreements into full-blown abuse. Moreover, the physical distance removes empathy cues; without seeing a victim's reaction, it becomes easier to dehumanize and disregard the hurt inflicted.

Online abuse takes diverse forms, each exploiting the unique affordances of digital platforms. *Public shaming* is often used to humiliate or ostracize an individual by broadcasting missteps or personal details to large audiences. *Threats* can range from vague intimidation to direct calls for violence, instilling fear and insecurity. More insidious are *coordinated attacks*, where groups organize to overwhelm a target with messages, reports, or harmful content, effectively silencing or drowning out dissenting voices. *Exclusion tactics* such as "cancel culture" can isolate and marginalize individuals by cutting them off from digital communities. These forms demonstrate how digital spaces, ostensibly designed for connection, can be weaponized to divide and harm.

The psychological consequences for victims of online harassment are profound and often enduring. Repeated exposure to hostility online can trigger *anxiety*, leaving victims fearful and hypervigilant when engaging in digital environments. *Depression* frequently follows, especially as harassment undermines self-esteem and erodes feelings of safety. Some individuals experience *trauma* comparable to that from offline abuse, resulting in symptoms such as nightmares, flashbacks, or social withdrawal. The blurred boundaries between online and offline life mean that digital abuse often permeates into real-world stress, affecting overall well-being. For many, the emotional toll is compounded by the sense of helplessness in confronting an often faceless and relentless adversary.

Observers of online harassment—the *bystanders*—play a crucial yet understudied role. Some choose silence, inadvertently enabling abuse through inaction or passive approval. Others provide *support* to victims by speaking out, offering solidarity, or reporting offenders. The response of bystanders can influence the dynamics of harassment, either curbing escalation or intensifying conflict. Moreover, witnessing harassment can provoke vicarious distress, making online spaces hostile not only to direct targets but also to the wider community. Encouraging empathetic and active bystander behavior remains a vital component of combating online abuse.

In response to the growing prevalence of harassment, social platforms have developed various *mechanisms* aimed at mitigation. *Reporting tools* allow users to flag abusive content, initiating review processes that may lead to content removal or sanctioning of offenders. *Blocking features* provide individualized control, enabling users to prevent contact from specific accounts. More broadly, platforms employ *content moderation*, combining automated algorithms with human reviewers to identify and act upon harmful behaviors. Yet, these systems face challenges such as scale, contextual ambiguity, and balancing free expression with protection. While imperfect, these response tools are essential components of creating safer digital environments.

The legal and ethical landscape governing online

harassment is complex. Jurisdictional issues arise because digital content crosses borders instantaneously, complicating enforcement and prosecution. Liability concerns involve determining the responsibility of platforms for user-generated content and the limits of free speech versus harmful conduct. Various countries have enacted laws addressing cyberharassment, yet enforcement remains uneven, and victims often find legal remedies slow or inaccessible. Ethical debates persist over privacy, censorship, and the rights of both victims and alleged harassers. Navigating these challenges requires ongoing dialogue among lawmakers, platforms, and civil society.

For individuals subjected to online hostility, *support* and *coping strategies* are crucial. Practical steps include cultivating strong social networks offline and online, seeking professional counseling, and employing digital tools such as filters to limit exposure. Learning to disengage from abusive interactions without internalizing negative messages aids emotional recovery. Various organizations and hotlines provide resources tailored to digital harassment victims, emphasizing that recovery is possible and that individuals are not alone. Empowering users with resilience and assistance helps mitigate the personal cost of online abuse.

Prevention blends psychology and technology through smart *design features*. Platforms now implement *filters* that detect patterns of harassment or flagged keywords, reducing abusive content before it reaches victims. *Artificial intelligence* tools increasingly assist moderators in scaling oversight efforts, though they must be carefully calibrated to avoid overreach or bias. Clear, enforceable *community guidelines* set behavioral expectations, promoting respect and accountability. Cultivating positive online cultures is as critical as technological fixes, demanding cooperation among users, designers, and policymakers.

The impact of online harassment extends far beyond individual encounters. It shifts social norms, stifles open discourse, and can marginalize vulnerable voices, undermining the inclusive promise of the internet. For victims, the emotional scars are often hidden and long-lasting, influencing their willingness to participate in public life and digital culture. Societally, unchecked hostility corrodes trust and mutual respect essential for healthy communities. Recognizing and confronting online harassment is thus vital not only to protect individuals but to preserve the very fabric of participatory digital society.

4.4 Comparing Ourselves to Others

Humans have long gauged their own standing through the lens of others, a practice known as social comparison. In the age of social platforms, this instinct—once confined to face-to-face encounters—has become amplified, chronic, and often invisible. Every swipe, like, or scroll invites us to measure ourselves against a constant stream of peers, celebrities, and acquaintances. This section explores how these social comparisons shape our self-image and emotions, illuminating both the pitfalls and possibilities hidden in our digital mirrors.

One foundational aspect of social comparison is whether we look *upward* or *downward*. Upward comparison happens when we pit ourselves against those perceived as better off, more talented, or more successful. Encountering a friend's flawless vacation photos or a colleague's promotion, for example, might inspire admiration but also highlight our own perceived shortcomings. Downward comparison, by contrast, is the act of looking at those doing worse and feeling superior by comparison. On social platforms, this might mean feeling relieved that our lives are not as chaotic as a viral complaint or messy breakup. Both types shape self-evaluation, but with different emotional outcomes: upward comparison can either motivate or diminish self-worth, while downward comparison often boosts ego, sometimes at the expense of empathy or growth.

A critical complicating factor on social media is the prevalence of *highlight reels*—carefully curated snapshots designed to impress. Profiles, posts, and stories tend to showcase polished personas rather than everyday reality. Rather than a truthful portrait, social platforms often present a veneer of perfection: the carefully filtered selfie, the trophy moment, or the smiling family dinner. This editorial control leads many users to compare themselves to unrealistic standards, fostering a sense of inadequacy. When the world's successes are pitched as effortlessly attainable, it can warp our perceptions and deepen dissatisfaction. An entire cottage industry of image crafting influences which moments get shared and which remain hidden, making comparison an uneven battleground where appearances often trump authenticity.

Layered onto this is the growing importance of *metrics-based comparison*. Unlike in-person encounters, social platforms offer quantifiable status indicators: follower counts, likes, comments, and shares. These statistics become shorthand for popularity, influence, or social capital. A post with hundreds of likes signals approval; a friend with thousands of followers commands an enviable audience. Such numeric evaluations encourage users to assess not just *who* is better off but *by how much*. This quantification can intensify emotions ranging from pride to anxiety, as users seek validation through engagement metrics or feel invisible when theirs are lacking. Over time, these numbers can supplant richer aspects of identity, reducing social worth to a tally displayed on a screen.

Another subtle but potent form of self-evaluation is *temporal self-comparison*—measuring the present self against one's past posts or achievements. Social platforms create record books of personal history, from childhood photos to last year's milestones. While reflecting on growth can be affirming, it can also trigger regret or nostalgia tinged with sadness. For instance, someone might scroll back to an earlier post brimming with optimism, only to feel disappointed by where life has since taken them. Temporal comparison invites a complex interplay of pride, loss, and aspiration. The permanence of online footprints can make moving on from past selves difficult and intensify feelings of stagnation or personal failure.

These comparison processes often evoke emotional responses with significant consequences. *Envy* and *jealousy* are among the most common reactions to perceived social inferiority. Envy arises from desiring something that others possess—be it beauty, success, or lifestyle—while jealousy involves fear of losing one's own valued relationships to others. Persistent upward comparison frequently fuels these feelings, which, if unacknowledged, can escalate into anxiety or depressive symptoms. Studies link heavy social media consumption with increased rates of loneliness and depression, partly driven by the constant bombardment of idealized images and stories that trigger feelings of inadequacy. These emotions are not inevitable but can be powerful enough to affect mental health, self-esteem, and social behaviors.

Central to many comparisons on social platforms are issues of *body image and lifestyle satisfaction*. The

105

omnipresence of idealized physical appearances—slim figures, flawless skin, and fashion trends—can distort users' perceptions of their own attractiveness. Beyond appearance, curated portrayals of achievements, luxury, and social success can create pressure to align with unattainable lifestyles. This mismatch can diminish satisfaction with one's own life circumstances and choices. The resulting discontent spills over into holistic well-being, influencing everything from eating behaviors and exercise habits to career ambitions and relationship expectations. For vulnerable populations, especially adolescents, these pressures contribute to heightened risks of body dissatisfaction and eating disorders.

The effects of social comparison, however, are not uniform across all users. *Cultural and demographic moderators* play a crucial role in shaping experiences online. Age differences, for example, influence comparison tendencies: younger users are often more susceptible to peer influence and image concerns, while older users may draw more on temporal comparisons connected to life milestones. Gender also mediates responses; women, especially teenage girls, show heightened sensitivity to appearance-based comparisons, while men may focus more on achievement or status indicators. Cultural backgrounds inform which social values and norms users emphasize, such as collectivist cultures where harmony and group success trump individual accolades. Recognizing these moderators helps explain why two users exposed to identical content may experience vastly different emotional responses.

Despite the risks, there are effective ways to mitigate the negative impact of comparison through *coping and resilience strategies*. Cognitive reframing encourages users to challenge assumptions embedded in comparison—for example, reminding oneself that social media highlights are not the full story behind others' lives. Media literacy skills involve critically analyzing content, identifying manipulation or exaggeration, and cultivating a more skeptical perspective toward polished images. Self-compassion practices help users respond to perceived shortcomings with kindness rather than harsh self-judgment. Additionally, setting boundaries around social media usage—such as limiting time or curating feeds—can reduce exposure to triggering comparisons. These tools foster greater psychological resilience and promote healthier online experiences.

Moreover, social comparison is not inherently detrimental. *Positive uses of comparison* emerge when individuals harness their observations to fuel inspiration, learning, and goal setting. Seeing a peer's success can motivate someone to develop new skills or pursue aspirations with renewed vigor. Upward comparison can illuminate achievable standards and pathways for personal development rather than merely spotlight deficits. When grounded in realistic appraisal and balanced emotions, comparison becomes a catalyst for growth and self-improvement rather than despair. It can ignite curiosity about others' journeys and expand perspectives on what might be possible.

Ultimately, social comparison on digital platforms is a double-edged sword, driving both promise and peril. It remains a fundamental human process that, depending on context and mindset, can enhance self-understanding or undermine well-being. By illuminating how we compare ourselves—upward and downward, to others and to our past—this exploration reveals the complexity beneath the surface of everyday scrolling. A deeper awareness of these mechanics empowers us not only to navigate the challenges of social media but also to reclaim our sense of self amid the curated façades and metrics-driven pages that now frame much of modern social life.

4.5 Digital Well-being and Mindful Use

In an age where digital connections often outnumber face-to-face interactions, maintaining a healthy relationship with social media is both a vital and delicate art. *Digital well-being* refers to the balance between engaging with online platforms and preserving one's mental, emotional, and social health. It acknowledges that while digital tools offer unparalleled access to information, entertainment, and community, excessive or unreflective use can lead to anxiety, distraction, and fatigue. Rather than asking us to abandon technology, digital well-being invites us to cultivate a more intentional, conscious engagement with it, where technology serves our values rather than enslaves our attention.

At its core, mindful consumption on social media challenges the habitual scrolling that so often dominates our digital diets. Mindfulness in this context means bringing awareness to how, why, and when we use these platforms. This practice involves noticing the emotional responses triggered by content, becoming aware of moments of distraction, and intentionally choosing the timing and manner of online interactions. Techniques such as brief pauses before opening an app, or reflecting on the purpose of a social media session, help convert passive consumption into an active, considered experience. For example, asking oneself, "Am I scrolling because I want to learn, connect, or simply out of boredom?" can enlighten usage habits and reduce unconscious overindulgence.

Technological solutions also play a role in supporting mindful use. Many smartphones and apps now include built-in *time management tools* like usage dashboards, screen time reports, and app timers that provide a clear picture of where digital minutes go. These tools allow users to set limits on daily use or restrict notifications during certain hours. Notification batching is another effective strategy, wherein notifications are collected and delivered at designated intervals instead of instantly, reducing constant distractions and helping preserve focus. By harnessing such features, users gain a structured form of self-regulation that complements personal awareness with tangible boundaries.

Equally important is the optimization of digital interfaces and environments to protect emotional balance. Settings such as *dark mode* reduce eye strain and blue-light exposure, which can interfere with sleep patterns. Implementing *quiet hours*—periods when notifications are muted—creates pockets of uninterrupted time essential for relaxation and deeper focus. Thoughtful design choices within apps, such as turning off autoplay videos or disabling infinite scroll features, can minimize compulsive behavior and reduce overstimulation. Small adjustments in the digital environment thus translate into meaningful improvements in mood and cognitive well-being.

Beyond these incremental changes lies the philosophy of *digital minimalism*. Rooted in the idea that "less is more," digital minimalism advocates for streamlining one's online engagements by focusing on a curated set of platforms and applications that deliver the highest personal value. This involves critical reflection about which digital tools truly enrich one's life and letting go of those that do not. For instance, instead of attempting to keep up with every trending app, a digital minimalist might choose one or two social networks that foster genuine connections or support professional growth. This selective approach reduces clutter and cognitive overload, ultimately freeing up time and mental space for what genuinely matters.

The practice of scheduled breaks and occasional digital detoxes further reinforces this balance. These deliberate pauses from connectivity—ranging from several hours each day to full days offline—offer crucial opportunities to recharge. Digital detoxes are not simply about abstention but about rediscovering life beyond screens: the texture of a book's pages, the rhythm of a walk, or the depth of a face-to-face conversation. These experiences replenish emotional reserves and sharpen one's awareness for returning to digital spaces with renewed intention and control.

Indeed, offline connections remain central to well-being despite the digital age's growing dominance. Human beings are inherently social creatures, wired for embodied, face-to-face interaction that conveys nuance and empathy beyond what screens can capture. Making time for in-person conversations, shared activities, and physical presence nurtures emotional resilience and combats the loneliness that can sometimes accompany online isolation. Rather than viewing digital interactions as substitutes, we benefit from integrating them as complements to rich, grounded social lives.

Forming and sustaining healthy digital habits hinges on principles of *habit formation and cue control*. Behavioral science shows that habits are triggered by contextual cues—such as a notification sound or a particular time of day—and sustained through repetition. To build mindful routines, it helps to redesign the environment to reduce tempting cues (for example, silencing phone notifications or placing devices out of immediate reach) and to replace automatic behaviors with deliberate alternatives, like taking deep breaths before unlocking an app. Over time, these small behavioral shifts accumulate, rewiring automatic responses into conscious practices aligned with well-being.

Purposeful engagement with social media amplifies these efforts by infusing online time with meaning beyond passive consumption. Using platforms for learning new skills, participating in constructive dialogues, or contributing to community initiatives fosters satisfaction and counters feelings of emptiness or comparison fatigue. For example, following educational channels, joining interest-based groups, or supporting nonprofit campaigns transforms digital usage into an active, values-driven pursuit. This purposefulness also encourages users to evaluate their feed critically, curating content that uplifts rather than diminishes mood.

Ultimately, cultivating digital well-being combines self-awareness, technological tools, conscious design, and intentional habit-building. Key practices include setting clear limits on screen time, creating distraction-free environments, embracing digital minimalism, scheduling regular offline intervals, and prioritizing meaningful offline relationships. By aligning digital engagement with one's values and emotional needs, individuals reclaim agency over their time and attention, transforming technology from a source of stress into a tool of enrichment.

This balanced approach encourages a rhythm of use that respects natural rhythms of focus and rest, leisure and connection. In doing so, it nurtures not only healthier online experiences but a more harmonious relationship with the digital world and oneself.

111

4.6 Mental Health Resources and Support

The journey toward psychological well-being is rarely solitary. Whether navigating mild stress or profound crises, access to the right resources can make a pivotal difference. Today's landscape offers an unprecedented array of tools and communities—both online and offline—that create webs of support tailored to diverse needs and preferences. This section unpacks these resources to help readers discern, engage with, and benefit from them effectively.

At the heart of many support networks lie *peer support communities*. These are moderated forums and group spaces where individuals share experiences, coping strategies, and encouragement. Unlike traditional therapy, peer groups provide a unique sense of belonging: the reassurance that one is not alone in their struggles. Platforms such as moderated online forums dedicated to anxiety, depression, or grief create safe environments where empathy flourishes without judgment. Communities like these can also be found in local settings, such as support groups organized through community centers or healthcare providers. The moderation is crucial—it ensures conversations remain respectful, informative, and free from misinformation or harmful advice, balancing openness with responsibility.

Parallel to peer support are *professional teletherapy services*, which have transformed the accessibility of licensed mental health care. Advances in technology enable users to connect with certified therapists via video calls, phone, or secure chat platforms, breaking down geographical and scheduling barriers. Services like BetterHelp, Talkspace, or regional equivalents offer flexible options for connecting with psychologists, counselors, and social workers. The implications are significant: people in remote areas, those with mobility issues, or those who prefer privacy can now receive consistent, personalized therapeutic guidance from home. Importantly, these platforms often incorporate intake assessments and matched provider systems, ensuring users find compatible professionals suited to their unique concerns.

Yet mental health challenges don't always arrive on a convenient timetable. For urgent situations, *crisis hotlines and emergency protocols* provide lifelines that operate 24/7. Organizations such as the National Suicide Prevention Lifeline, Samaritans, or Crisis Text Line respond to immediate distress, offering compassionate listening, risk assessment, and emergency intervention referrals. These helplines can serve as crucial first steps during moments of overwhelming despair, suicidal thoughts, or acute anxiety attacks. Knowing the numbers and procedures tailored to one's location—often available through government or NGO websites—empowers individuals and families to act decisively in crises, potentially saving lives.

Complementing these human-to-human interactions are *self-help apps and digital interventions*, which harness technology to support mental health maintenance day to day. These apps come in many forms: mood trackers that map emotional fluctuations over time, guided meditation sessions rooted in mindfulness practice, and cognitive behavioral therapy (CBT) tools designed to challenge negative thought patterns. Popular apps like Headspace, Calm, or Moodpath offer accessible ways to develop coping skills, relax, and build resilience. Their appeal lies in immediacy and user control—allowing users to engage discreetly and at their own pace. Nonetheless, since these apps vary in scientific backing and design quality, discerning users should apply careful judgment before relying exclusively on such tools.

Closely tied to app usage are *privacy and confidentiality considerations*, paramount when personal mental health data is involved. Digital platforms must adhere to stringent data protection standards—such as HIPAA in the United States or GDPR in Europe—to secure sensitive information from misuse or breaches. Users should prioritize services that clearly disclose their privacy policies, encryption methods, and data-sharing practices. Additionally, understanding what constitutes anonymized versus identifiable data can influence comfort levels with different tools. In online peer communities, while anonymity can encourage honesty and openness, it may also raise challenges for moderation and safety. Hence, transparent moderation policies and user controls are critical to maintaining trust.

Beyond standalone apps, many online platforms now incorporate *in-app mental health initiatives*—partnerships with mental health organizations that embed resource hubs and crisis support directly into social media, gaming, or general wellness apps. Instagram and TikTok, for example, provide links to helplines and educational content when users engage with certain hashtags or search queries related to depression or anxiety. These initiatives reflect growing recognition of mental health as a public concern and use the reach and immediacy of digital platforms to connect users with appropriate help. Similarly, workplace wellness apps often integrate mental health resources within broader corporate health programs, normalizing support and reducing stigma in professional settings.

114

Access to reliable information is a foundational pillar for well-being, which underscores the value of *educational and psychoeducational content*. Numerous blogs, webinars, podcasts, and online courses provide scientifically informed insights into mental health topics—ranging from stress management and emotional regulation to trauma recovery and mindfulness practices. Organizations like the National Alliance on Mental Illness (NAMI), Mental Health America, or WHO offer free, accessible content designed to enhance understanding and promote proactive care. These resources enable users to become informed advocates for their own health or that of loved ones, bridging the gap between lay knowledge and clinical expertise.

As powerful as these resources can be is the importance of *building supportive online networks* with intention. Positive communities arise when participants follow best practices that prioritize empathy, validate differing experiences, and avoid harm. Clear community guidelines, active moderation, and skills in compassionate listening foster environments where difficult conversations can unfold without triggering exclusion or stigma. Encouraging users to share stories while respecting boundaries contributes to resilience, while emphasizing strengths and recovery aligns focus towards hope. Such networks often ripple beyond the digital world, catalyzing peer-led initiatives, advocacy, or in-person meetups that deepen social connection.

Navigating this diverse ecosystem requires tools for *evaluating resource credibility*. Not all support platforms or materials are created equal. Critical criteria include qualifications and licensure of professionals involved; evidence or research underpinning app techniques; transparency of organizational sponsorship; user reviews combined with expert endorsements; and clear guidelines for privacy and ethical standards. An informed consumer sustains their well-being best by balancing open-mindedness with healthy skepticism—seeking resources that demonstrate accountability and effectiveness rather than mere popularity.

Taken together, these avenues outline a mosaic of *support pathways* that cater to different stages and intensities of mental health needs. From informal peer conversations and self-directed tools to real-time crisis help and professional therapeutic engagement, the options are vast and complementary. The challenge—and opportunity—lies in recognizing when and how to use various mechanisms, adapting over time as circumstances evolve. This empowers individuals not only to weather challenges but to cultivate ongoing mental wellness, ultimately weaving psychological support seamlessly into the fabric of everyday life.

Chapter 5

Social Media in Education and Learning

This chapter examines the transformative role of social media in both formal and informal learning environments. We begin by exploring how platforms foster collaborative communities and peer support, then assess the wealth of educational content accessible online. Next, we analyze strategies for boosting student engagement and participation, followed by the evolving professional networks that support educators. We then address the risks of distraction and academic dishonesty, and conclude by defining the digital literacy competencies learners need to thrive in the social media era.

5.1 Learning Communities and Peer Support

Understanding how knowledge flourishes in social settings requires us first to consider the powerful learning theories that foreground interaction as the seedbed of understanding. Social constructivism, pioneered by thinkers like Lev Vygotsky, asserts that learners construct knowledge through dialogue and shared experiences rather than through isolated study. Complementing this, the more recent theory of connectivism proposed by George Siemens emphasizes the formation of networks, where learning emerges from the interplay of diverse nodes—people, databases, and digital resources—connected through technology. Together, these frameworks illuminate why social platforms are not mere communication tools but dynamic ecosystems fostering collaborative knowledge creation.

Modern digital spaces have become fertile ground for these ideas to take shape, offering environments where study groups are no longer confined to physical classrooms or meeting rooms. Platforms such as Facebook Groups, Discord servers, and Slack channels have emerged as popular hubs for learners seeking peer support. Facebook Groups, with their familiarity and broad user base, allow communities centered around specific subjects or courses to thrive, offering threaded discussions and file sharing that bind members in collective pursuit. Discord servers, originally designed for gamers, now attract educational communities drawn by their real-time voice and text channels that simulate an ever-present study lounge, complete with informal conversation alongside focused work. Slack, favored in professional and academic contexts, structures interactions via channels and direct messaging, enabling organized, topic-specific conversations and easy integration with other productivity tools.

The architecture of these platforms is essential to their success. Discussion threads and channel hierarchies transform the chaos of conversation into ordered knowledge streams. In Facebook Groups, posts spawn nested comment threads where questions, answers, and clarifications weave a layered tapestry of learning, allowing newcomers to catch up without wading through irrelevant chatter. Discord and Slack extend this idea with channels dedicated to particular subjects or tasks—imagine a "Calculus Help" channel, an "Exam Strategies" corner, or a "Paper Review" room— each a mini-forum where focused dialogue unfolds uninterrupted. Such organization respects both the breadth and depth of topics, helping communities prevent the common pitfall of disorganized discussion, which can drown valuable insights.

Collaborative document editing has revolutionized the very act of producing shared work. Tools like Google Docs and OneDrive enable multiple users to co-author assignments, brainstorm collectively, or compile notes in real time. The magic lies not just in simultaneous typing but in the visible trace of each contributor's input, fostering transparency and a sense of joint ownership. Collaborative editing tools reduce the friction that once accompanied group work, dissolving geographical and temporal barriers. They invite a fluid, iterative approach to knowledge-building, where drafts evolve through ongoing interaction, corrections, and refinements—processes that are inherently social and deeply educational.

Beyond documents, social annotation tools such as Hypothes.is invite learners to engage directly with texts in a communal fashion. By allowing groups to highlight passages, add margin notes, and pose questions anchored to specific sections of a reading, these platforms turn passive consumption into active dialogue. The annotation layers become a collective commentary, fostering deeper engagement and enabling subtle peer teaching moments. This approach mirrors traditional study circles crowding around a book, yet scales effortlessly to encompass participants scattered across different continents, all interacting synchronously or asynchronously.

Peer feedback and scaffolding represent the crucial

social glue that makes collaborative learning thrive. When learners comment on drafts, respond to questions, or offer constructive criticism, they provide scaffolds—temporary supports that enable peers to reach higher levels of understanding than they might alone. Comments, reactions, and even simple "likes" signal encouragement and direction, creating iterative feedback loops where work is progressively improved. This peer-driven refinement not only enhances the product but deepens the learner's own grasp of content and processes, an effect well-documented in education research.

Yet, managing vibrant online learning communities demands thoughtful facilitation and moderation. Skilled facilitators set clear norms around communication, encourage respectful dialogue, and model constructive behavior. They intervene when discussions veer off course or become contentious, safeguarding an environment where all feel welcome to contribute. Sustaining engagement over time requires creativity— polls, weekly challenges, spotlight posts featuring member contributions, or synchronous study sessions can energize participation. Moderators also track group health: Are newcomers welcomed? Are resources accessible? Is the group achieving its learning goals? Their role evolves from gatekeepers to cultivators of collaborative culture.

Despite best efforts, participation inequality is a persistent challenge. Online communities often reveal a "90-9-1" pattern: 90% lurk silently, 9% contribute occasionally, and 1% dominate discussions. This imbalance risks muffling diverse voices and limits the full richness of collective intelligence. Strategies to counteract this include creating low-stakes opportunities for input, such as polls or micro-contributions, assigning rotating roles like discussion leader or summarizer, and directly inviting quieter members to share thoughts in smaller groups. Recognizing and valuing all forms of engagement helps transform silent observers into active learners and strengthens community resilience.

One instructive example is an online study group formed around a popular massive open online course (MOOC) on data science. The group utilized a dedicated Discord server segmented into channels by topic—statistics, machine learning, visualization—and incorporated Google Docs for collaborative note-taking and project development. Crucially, the group appointed peer moderators who scheduled regular "office hours" sessions, during which more experienced learners facilitated live Q&A and code reviews. Social annotation tools were leveraged to dissect reading assignments collectively. Over twelve weeks, members reported higher course completion rates and a deeper understanding of complex concepts compared to working alone. The group's success rested on transparent roles, clear norms, and a culture prioritizing peer support over competition.

In building and sustaining learning communities, key principles emerge: social interaction is the lifeblood of knowledge formation; technology must support organization rather than overwhelm participants; shared creation benefits from visible, iterative feedback; and facilitators play a vital role in nurturing inclusive, active spaces. By embracing these elements, learners transform scattered individuals into interconnected networks, tapping into the collective power of their peers and turning education into a richly social endeavor.

5.2 Access to Educational Content

The explosion of digital platforms has transformed how we access knowledge, dissolving once insurmountable barriers of location, cost, and time. Social media and on-line tools now offer a rich, sprawling universe of educational content, ranging from fully-fledged courses to bite-sized lessons and curated collections. This wide spectrum invites learners of all ages and backgrounds to discover, engage with, and even contribute to learning materials in new and dynamic ways.

Central to this shift are *Open Educational Resources* (OER), which represent freely available textbooks, courses, lesson plans, and multimedia materials anyone can use, adapt, and share. Unlike traditional copyrighted content locked behind paywalls or institutional access, OER democratize learning by stripping away financial and legal obstacles. Platforms such as OpenStax and the Creative Commons repository anchor a growing ecosystem of high-quality, peer-reviewed resources fashioned by educators and institutions committed to open sharing. This ethos not only broadens access but encourages local adaptation, enabling educators worldwide to tailor materials for cultural relevance and language.

Building on open content, *Massive Open Online Courses* (MOOCs) integrate formalized instruction with social learning features. Providers like Coursera, edX, and FutureLearn combine video lectures with discussion forums, peer assessments, and collaborative projects. These social elements encourage dialogue among thousands of learners globally, replicating some dynamics of a physical classroom and fostering a community-driven spirit. For example, debate threads and study groups help demystify complex subjects, while peer review mechanisms promote critical thinking and feedback. Thus, MOOCs evolve beyond passive lectures into interactive ecosystems where knowledge grows through participation.

Complementing MOOCs, *video tutorials and channels* populate platforms like YouTube and Vimeo, forming accessible, informal hubs of expertise on nearly any topic imaginable. Channels operated by educators, hobbyists, and experts include everything from cooking and coding to advanced science and philosophy. Their appeal lies in immediacy and flexibility—learners can jump directly to brief how-to videos or immerse themselves in comprehensive series. The algorithms behind these platforms often recommend tailored content based on viewing habits, subtly guiding learners through ever-deepening journeys. For instance, a beginner guitar player might start with a basics tutorial, then receive suggestions for advanced techniques or music theory lessons, all within a single digital space.

In a further refinement, *microlearning* has found fertile ground on social apps like TikTok, Instagram Stories, and Snapchat. These platforms deliver extremely short, focused lessons—often under a minute—that fit neatly into busy schedules. Popular educators, scientists, language tutors, and historians harness the format's visual and narrative brevity to distill complex ideas into memorable snippets. The power of microlearning lies not only in accessibility but in creative engagement: quick quizzes, challenges, and visual storytelling turn passive scrolling into active, playful learning moments. This innovation highlights how educational content adapts to evolving attention spans and device preferences without sacrificing substance.

Not all learning depends on visuals, however. *Podcasts and audio lessons* have carved a distinct niche by enabling

123

education during commutes, exercise, or chores. Their popularity stems from combining storytelling, interviews, and expert dialogues that engage listeners through sound alone. Educational podcasts, from language instruction to history deep dives, offer flexible, on-the-go learning unattainable through conventional text or video. Moreover, platforms like Spotify and Apple Podcasts include features like episode playlists and transcription, allowing learners to integrate listening with other media formats seamlessly.

As the volume of digital learning content grows, effective *content curation and playlists* become essential tools. Learners often rely on creating personalized collections—playlists on YouTube, RSS feed aggregators, or bookmarked resource libraries—to organize and revisit valuable materials. Curation empowers individuals to impose order on the sprawling digital landscape, crafting coherent pathways through diverse content. For example, a student of world history might assemble sources in chronological order, blending videos, articles, and podcasts, tailoring the journey to specific interests or syllabus requirements. Social media also facilitates communal curation, as groups share recommendations or collaborative lists that enrich collective learning.

The global nature of online education raises questions of language accessibility. Fortunately, advances in *multilingual content and translation* technologies have expanded the reach of materials far beyond their original linguistic borders. Automatic captioning, machine translation, and community-driven subtitling projects enable learners to access content in their native languages or follow along using translated transcripts. This inclusivity widens participation and respects cultural diversity, connecting knowledge seekers worldwide. It also invites contributions from non-English speakers, creating a virtuous cycle where more languages enrich the educational commons.

Equally critical are built-in *accessibility features* that support learners with disabilities or different needs. Captioning, transcripts, alt text for images, and screen-reader compatibility transform social platforms from mere content repositories into truly inclusive environments. For example, a deaf learner can grasp video lessons through accurate captions, while someone with visual impairment benefits from descriptive audio or text. Accessibility improvements ensure that the diversity of human experience is accommodated, reinforcing the democratizing mission of digital education.

Alongside content breadth and accessibility, new forms of *credentialing* have emerged to recognize and validate the skills learners acquire. *Micro-credentials* and digital badges offered through MOOCs, certification platforms, and even some social networks provide portable, verifiable evidence of achievement. Unlike traditional diplomas, these credentials often focus on specific skills or project outcomes and can be shared easily on professional networks like LinkedIn. They serve not only as motivation but as currency in job markets increasingly responsive to lifelong learning and specialized expertise. Although still evolving in acceptance and rigor, micro-credentials symbolize a shift toward more flexible, learner-centered validation.

Together, these developments illustrate how social media and related tools have vastly expanded, diversified, and organized access to educational content. From open textbooks and MOOCs to viral micro-lessons and community-curated playlists, learners no longer face a one-size-fits-all model but a customizable landscape where discovery and participation coalesce. Language inclusiveness and accessibility features further widen the circle, ensuring that learning can genuinely be for everyone. Meanwhile, digital badges and micro-credentials help translate knowledge into recognized competencies, closing the loop between acquisition and application.

The educational terrain shaped by social platforms is vibrant and constantly evolving, blending technology, pedagogy, and social interaction. It challenges traditional institutions and offers unprecedented agency to learners, who are now empowered to seek, assemble, and certify knowledge on their own terms. This new ecosystem invites curiosity, creativity, and connection—hallmarks not only of modern education but of an informed, engaged society.

5.3 Student Engagement and Participation

Understanding student engagement is crucial for transforming passive consumption of information into active learning experiences, especially within digital environments where distractions abound. At its core, engagement unfolds across three intertwined dimensions: behavioral, emotional, and cognitive. *Behavioral engagement* refers to the observable actions students take—logging in, completing assignments, participating in discussions, or using interactive tools. *Emotional engagement* captures the feelings and attitudes learners bring to the process—whether they find the material interesting, feel connected to peers, or are motivated to persist. *Cognitive engagement* delves deeper into mental investment, reflecting how students reflect on content, strategize their learning, and apply critical thinking. Digital platforms must encourage all three to create a holistic, vibrant learning experience.

To kindle and sustain active learner involvement, many online education environments harness *gamification elements*—design features borrowed from games that engender motivation and enjoyment. Points reward accomplishments, badges symbolize milestones, leaderboards introduce friendly competition, and progress bars visually track advancement. For instance, a course might award points for completing quizzes or posting insightful comments, turning a potentially solitary activity into a stimulating challenge. This approach leverages our innate desire for achievement and recognition, nudging students toward continued participation without trivializing content. However, it requires careful calibration to avoid reducing learning to a mere quest for rewards.

Another potent tool for interaction is the use of *live polls and Q&A* sessions integrated into synchronous or asynchronous lectures. Platforms such as Mentimeter allow instructors to pose real-time questions, quizzes, or opinion polls that students answer instantly, embedding active response within the flow of teaching. This not only breaks monotony but generates a sense of shared inquiry. Embedded social polls, meanwhile, provide avenues for reflective feedback, revealing gaps in understanding and guiding instructional adjustments. These techniques empower learners to influence the pace and direction of their education, creating an inclusive dialogue rather than a monologue.

Complementing these interactive tools is the concept of *backchannel communication*, where parallel conversations unfold alongside formal lessons. Students might tweet using a specific hashtag or participate in a Slack thread dedicated to course topics, voicing questions, sharing resources, or commenting on peers' remarks in real time. Such backchannels have democratizing potential, allowing quieter students to express thoughts without interrupting the classroom rhythm and fostering community beyond the official syllabus. At its best, this dynamic creates a digital agora—a lively marketplace of ideas enhancing engagement through immediacy and collective exchange.

When it comes to building knowledge collaboratively, *collaborative note-taking* stands out as a particularly effective strategy. Shared documents, wikis, or cloud-based notebooks enable groups of students to co-create summaries, highlight key concepts, and pose questions. This collective effort not only distributes cognitive load but encourages negotiation of meaning—students must decide what to include, how to phrase ideas, and how to connect them. Such collaboration turns passive note-taking into an active process of meaning-making and reflection, reinforcing learning while building a sense of shared ownership and responsibility.

Extending reflection beyond immediate interactions, *reflective blogging and vlogging* offer students a platform to document their learning journeys in richer, more personal forms. Writing blogs or producing video journals prompts learners to articulate thoughts, synthesize ideas, and examine their evolving understanding. These student-generated artifacts serve as evidence of engagement and authenticity, revealing not only what learners know but how they think and feel about their learning. Moreover, sharing these reflections with a wider audience cultivates skills in communication and critical self-assessment, essential for lifelong learning.

Peer-to-peer teaching further deepens engagement by positioning students as knowledge creators and leaders.

When learners develop tutorials, lead mini-workshops, or explain concepts to classmates, they solidify their own comprehension and instill confidence. This strategy also fosters a supportive community where expertise is distributed rather than centralized, benefiting both "teacher" and "student." By actively constructing and transmitting knowledge, students move from passive recipients to active participants, embodying the principle that to teach is to learn twice.

Behind the scenes, sophisticated *engagement analytics* offer educators and institutions valuable insights into interactive behaviors. Dashboards track metrics such as frequency of posts, participation rates in discussions, time spent on activities, and responsiveness to peer comments. These data-driven snapshots help identify who is truly involved and who may be superficially present, enabling timely interventions and personalized support. While numbers can never capture the full depth of engagement, they provide an important lens to better understand patterns and optimize learning environments.

However, the rise of digital platforms also brings challenges, especially the risk of *superficial engagement*. The culture of "likes," quick reactions, and surface-level interactions can create an illusion of involvement without deeper cognitive or emotional commitment. A student might click "like" or scroll through content without internalizing it, mistaking activity for learning. Recognizing this, educators must differentiate between quantity and quality of engagement, cultivating habits that promote meaningful reflection and critical thinking rather than mere performance for the platform's sake.

Combining these approaches yields a rich palette of participation strategies that foster genuine student involvement. Techniques such as gamification capture

129

interest and motivate sustained interaction; live polls and backchannel discussions generate real-time dialogue and inclusivity; collaborative note-taking and peer teaching encourage active knowledge building; reflective blogging nurtures metacognition; and engagement analytics enable evidence-based refinement. Mindful of superficial engagement, educators can blend these elements to create environments where students not only engage but thrive—actively shaping their journey toward deeper understanding and lasting learning.

5.4 Teacher Presence and Professional Networks

In an era where connectivity is as essential as chalk and blackboards once were, educators have found fertile ground in cultivating their digital professional identities. Beyond the classroom walls, teachers now craft public personas online that balance authenticity with professionalism, signaling expertise while inviting collaboration. This digital presence is not merely self-promotion; it represents a thoughtful construction of who an educator is in an interconnected landscape—where a tweet can spark pedagogical innovation and a blog post might reshape instructional practices globally.

Crafting a digital professional identity involves blending personal voice with professional expertise. Educators share insights, reflect on classroom experiences, and contribute to conversations shaping education's future. Authenticity remains paramount; the identity must feel genuine and lived rather than a mere façade. For example, a high school history teacher tweeting critical questions about civic engagement or a math educator posting creative problem-solving strategies demonstrate how individuality and professionalism meld. Platforms like LinkedIn, Twitter, and educator-specific spaces such as Edmodo provide frameworks for these identities, but the essence lies in consistent, meaningful engagement that resonates with peers and students alike.

At the heart of these digital identities lie Professional Learning Networks (PLNs), dynamic communities where educators connect, exchange resources, and foster collective growth. Unlike traditional, geographically bound networks, PLNs transcend borders, making expertise accessible regardless of location. Twitter stands out as a vital hub, where hashtag-categorized discussions such as #EdChat enable educators worldwide to dive into real-time conversations on topics from literacy to technology integration. Similarly, Facebook groups and specialized forums cultivate niche communities; for instance, groups dedicated to STEM teaching or inclusive education facilitate targeted discourse and resource exchange. These networks embody the adage "learning is social," proving that professional growth thrives on interaction and community.

Resource sharing and curation form another cornerstone of teacher presence in the digital sphere. Teachers are both consumers and creators of educational materials, and social bookmarking tools have revolutionized how these resources are organized and disseminated. Platforms like Pinterest and Wakelet allow educators to compile themed collections—lesson plans, multimedia assets, or assessment ideas—making valuable materials accessible and reusable. Institutional repositories and open educational resources complement these personal collections, ensuring that high-quality content is preserved and shared within a trusted environment. This curated sharing enriches classroom practice, allowing teachers to stand on the shoulders of countless innovators while contributing their unique insights to the growing educational commons.

In weaving their networks, educators often embrace hashtag communities and Twitter chats, which punctuate the weekly rhythms of professional interaction. Scheduled chats—weekly or monthly gatherings online around trending or enduring educational themes—provide structured yet informal spaces for peer exchange. Whether discussing formative assessment strategies, classroom management, or equity in education, these chats invite diverse voices to converse, debate, and reflect. Hashtags not only organize content but also foster belonging, enabling educators to signal interests, build reputations, and connect with like-minded professionals. The immediacy and accessibility of this format facilitate spontaneous mentorship, resource dissemination, and collective problem-solving fueled by authentic dialogue.

Mentorship and peer coaching have found new vitality through digital connectivity. Direct messaging on platforms like Twitter, virtual meetups via Zoom, or informal group calls knit educators into support networks extending beyond institutional boundaries. These interactions provide personalized feedback, encouragement, and professional companionship vital for growth and resilience. For instance, a novice teacher might seek guidance in virtual office hours hosted by experienced mentors, while a network of teachers might collaboratively troubleshoot challenges in project-based learning. The ease of forming such ties online diminishes geographical constraints and democratizes access to expert advice, enriching professional development with immediacy and nuance.

The sphere of classroom social presence expands

these connections into students' learning environments. Teachers establish class blogs, Instagram feeds, or closed groups, using digital platforms to extend discussions, showcase student work, and build community beyond school hours. These spaces cultivate relationships, foster student voice, and invite families into the educational process. For example, a class Instagram account documenting science experiments or a blog reflecting on literature discussions enables learners to engage with content creatively and publicly. When managed thoughtfully, these tools nurture belonging and motivation, creating a seamless bridge between physical and virtual learning landscapes.

However, traversing this digital territory demands attentiveness to ethical boundaries and privacy. Maintaining student confidentiality and modeling professional conduct remain foundational responsibilities. Educators must negotiate the tension between transparency and discretion, ensuring that digital sharing does not compromise individual rights or professional integrity. This might mean anonymizing student data in shared resources, securing parental permissions before posting images or work samples, or refraining from expressing personal opinions that could undermine trust. Navigating these ethical challenges is critical to sustaining the credibility and safety of online educator presence.

Platform policies play an essential role in shaping the contours of teacher engagement. Acceptable use guidelines outline what sorts of interactions and content are appropriate, while copyright considerations govern the sharing and creation of educational materials. Awareness of these frameworks helps educators protect themselves and their students from breaches and legal pitfalls. For example, understanding fair use policies ensures that teachers can ethically incorporate multimedia resources without infringing on intellectual property. Similarly, safeguarding user safety—through secure passwords, privacy controls, and awareness of online risks—empowers educators to engage confidently and responsibly.

Continuous professional development intersects naturally with digital networks, leveraging webinars, micro-courses, and Massive Open Online Courses (MOOCs) tailored to educators' evolving needs. These flexible, accessible learning formats support upskilling in areas ranging from digital literacy to classroom management and innovative pedagogies. The asynchronous nature of many MOOCs allows teachers to engage at their own pace, while webinars provide live interaction and expert insights. Coupled with the social learning found in PLNs, these professional development opportunities form a rich ecosystem, propelling educators toward lifelong learning within a supportive community.

Together, these elements underscore the transformative potential of teacher presence and professional networks. They reveal how educators today are not solitary figures but active participants in vibrant, interconnected communities that nurture growth, creativity, and resilience. Building and sustaining these networks demands intentionality and balance: authenticity and professionalism, openness and caution, individual voice and collective wisdom. Through digital identities, resource curation, mentorship, and continuous development, educators harness the power of connection to enrich their practice, inspire their students, and shape the future of education itself.

5.5 Risks of Distraction and Plagiarism

Social media's infiltration into the academic landscape brings with it a double-edged dilemma: the ease of distraction and the temptation of dishonesty. While these platforms offer vast opportunities for connection and collaboration, their design and culture can also undermine the focus and integrity essential for genuine learning.

One of the most pervasive issues is *off-task browsing and attention fragmentation*. Social media platforms are engineered to capture and sustain user attention through endless scrolling and real-time notifications. During study sessions, the sudden buzz of a message or the lure of an infinite content feed can disrupt concentration, pulling students away from deep engagement with their work. Each interruption—be it a comment, an update, or a like—fragments attention into smaller, less productive bursts, and multiple studies have confirmed that frequent task-switching hinders comprehension and long-term retention. The result is a learning experience marked by shallow processing rather than meaningful absorption.

This fragmentation stands in stark contrast to what cognitive scientists term *deep work*—a state of focused, uninterrupted concentration critical for mastering complex material. Unlike multitasking, which nudges the brain to sporadically toggle between competing tasks, deep work enables sustained cognitive effort, fostering creativity and insight. Unfortunately, social media's constant stimuli encourage the illusion of productivity through multitasking, yet evidence shows this fragmented engagement reduces both the quality and efficiency of learning. Instead of thorough understanding, students often emerge with superficial familiarity, ill-prepared for critical thinking or problem-solving.

Alongside the distraction challenges is the darker issue of academic dishonesty facilitated by social media's networks and anonymity. *Cheating via shared answers* has become a modern phenomenon, where closed student groups or private messaging channels circulate solutions to assignments and exams. These virtual echo chambers often thrive on peer pressure or the convenience of instant access to answers, eroding the principle of individual effort. What might once have required clandestine meetings or secret notes now unfolds in public or semi-private digital spaces, making unethical collaboration disturbingly easy and widespread.

Even more insidious are the practices of *contract cheating and essay mills*, where students outsource their assignments to third-party services that promise original, custom-written work for a fee. These operations, often advertised and exchanged via social media, exploit the anonymity and global reach of the internet. Contract cheating strips away the educational value of assignments, replacing learning with transactional exchanges. The problem is compounded by the difficulty educators face in detecting such deception, especially as these purchased papers are tailored to individual prompts and styles.

In response, educators and institutions have adopted an arsenal of *detection tools and plagiarism checkers*. Platforms like Turnitin and Copyscape scan submitted work against vast databases of published material and student papers, flagging suspicious overlaps or copied text. These tools serve as frontline defenses against straightforward plagiarism, discouraging blatant copying by raising the likelihood of discovery.

However, they are less effective against more subtle forms of dishonesty, such as paraphrasing without citation or contract cheating, which require additional investigative tactics.

To further strengthen verification, *authorship verification methods* have grown in sophistication. Stylometry, the analysis of a writer's unique linguistic fingerprint—such as typical sentence length, vocabulary complexity, and punctuation usage—helps identify inconsistencies in submitted work that might indicate ghostwriting. Digital watermarking embeds invisible markers within text or code, revealing tampering or unauthorized reuse. These innovations reflect academia's evolving struggle to preserve authenticity in a digital era where texts can be easily bought, copied, or manipulated.

Yet technological solutions represent only part of the puzzle. Recognizing that the incentive structure drives much of the unethical behavior, educators increasingly turn to *assessment design strategies* to discourage cheating at its root. Open-book exams, project-based tasks, and reflective assignments emphasize process, understanding, and personal insight rather than rote memorization or one-size-fits-all answers. By requiring original thought and application, these formats make it harder to recycle generic solutions or outsource work. Moreover, they align more closely with real-world skills, fostering genuine competence over superficial achievement.

At the heart of these measures lie *academic integrity policies*, whose purpose extends beyond punishment to cultivate a culture of honesty and respect. Honor codes, detailed conduct guidelines, and transparent enforcement procedures establish clear expectations and consequences. When students buy into these principles, they are more likely to act ethically and view their learning as a personal and collective responsibility rather than a transactional game to be won or cheated.

Building such buy-in demands proactive *student education on ethics*. Integrity modules, peer pledges, and scenario-based training sessions help students recognize the value of honest work and the pitfalls of cutting corners. By engaging learners in discussions about fairness, trust, and long-term goals, educators create an environment where integrity becomes a shared norm rather than a set of rules to circumvent. This ethical awareness can also empower students to resist the peer pressure and convenience factors that social media often intensifies.

Together, these combined strategies aim to *synthesize risk mitigation* by both minimizing distractions and upholding honesty. Limiting off-task social media use during study times preserves the mental space needed for deep learning, while thoughtful assessment design and technological safeguards reduce opportunities and motivations for cheating. When supported by clear policies and ethical education, this multifaceted approach fosters an academic environment where focus and integrity reinforce one another rather than fall prey to the seductive but corrosive influences of social media.

Ultimately, the challenge is not to demonize social media outright but to acknowledge and manage its risks. The same platforms that threaten to fragment attention and encourage shortcuts also hold vast potential for collaboration, resource-sharing, and engagement when harnessed thoughtfully. Navigating this balance remains a task not only for educators and institutions but for every student striving to learn meaningfully in the digital age.

5.6 Digital Literacy as a Skill

Navigating social media is no longer a simple matter of scrolling and clicking; it demands a sophisticated set of competencies collectively known as digital literacy. At its core, digital literacy blends information literacy—the ability to locate and appraise information—with media literacy, which centers on understanding and producing media content, and technological literacy, the know-how of engaging with digital tools and platforms. In social media environs, these literacies intersect and amplify one another: users must interpret diverse content formats, scrutinize sources, and create responsible, meaningful contributions amid a whirl of ever-changing algorithms and social norms.

One foundational skill within digital literacy is the critical evaluation of sources. Unlike traditional media, where editorial oversight offers some assurance of quality, social platforms teem with content that varies wildly in accuracy and intent. To separate fact from fiction, savvy users employ techniques such as *lateral reading*, which involves cross-referencing information across multiple sites rather than remaining confined to a single one. This method reduces reliance on any one source and helps identify consensus or flag inconsistencies. Additionally, frameworks like the CRAAP test—assessing Currency, Relevance, Authority, Accuracy, and Purpose—provide concrete criteria to judge a source's trustworthiness. Applying these strategies habitually equips individuals to wade through misinformation and discern reliable data amid digital noise.

Yet credibility is only one piece of the puzzle. Equally critical is understanding the invisible architecture shaping what content users see. Social media platforms employ sophisticated recommendation engines that filter and prioritize posts, videos, and advertisements based on user behavior. These algorithms create what are often termed *filter bubbles*, personalized echo chambers that reinforce existing perspectives by preferentially exposing users to familiar ideas and contacts. Recognizing this phenomenon is key to fostering balanced worldviews and critical thinking. Awareness of algorithmic influence encourages deliberate actions such as diversifying content sources and questioning the perceived ubiquity or consensus of certain viewpoints.

Closely intertwined with these concerns is the management of privacy and digital footprints. Every interaction on social media—likes, shares, comments—leaves a trace that contributes to an enduring digital persona. Mastery of privacy controls, understanding password hygiene, and prudent judgments about data sharing form essential defense mechanisms against identity theft, targeted advertising, and surveillance. For instance, adjusting account settings to limit data visibility, using strong, unique passwords supplemented with two-factor authentication, and being cautious about linking multiple accounts help maintain control over personal information. Developing this awareness empowers users to safeguard their digital identities against misuse and maintain autonomy in online spaces.

Fluency in digital environments also requires familiarity with netiquette—the unwritten conventions that govern respectful and effective communication in the online realm. Social media demands attention to tone, clarity, and decorum, especially since absence of face-to-face cues can easily lead to misunderstandings. Ethical posting involves attributing quotes and images correctly, respecting copyright laws, and avoiding inflammatory or harmful language. Cultivating empathy and restraint contributes not only to individual reputation but also to healthier online communities, where dialogue and difference can coexist without devolving into hostility.

Competence extends beyond consumption to creation. Basic content creation skills—such as composing engaging posts, editing images for clarity and appeal, and crafting short videos with coherent narratives— are increasingly indispensable. These techniques enable users to express themselves authentically and effectively, whether promoting a cause, sharing personal stories, or participating in cultural conversations. Tools designed for ease of use democratize content production, turning passive viewers into active participants and collaborators in the digital age.

Data literacy underpins these creative endeavors by revealing patterns behind user engagement. Interpreting likes, shares, comments, and view metrics offers practical feedback on content impact and audience preferences. For learners and creators alike, basic visualization skills—such as plotting data trends or comparing demographic reach—enhance understanding of how content resonates. This analytical dimension transforms social media from a one-way broadcast into a dynamic interaction, where measurable outcomes inform future choices and strategies.

Concomitant with these literacies is cybersecurity awareness, a pillar of safe digital practices. Recognizing phishing attempts, avoiding malicious downloads, and adopting secure browsing habits shield users from common cyber threats. Cybercriminals frequently exploit social media's openness to distribute scams or malware, making vigilance crucial. Simple precautions—never clicking suspicious links, regularly updating software, and using reputable security tools—form the frontline of defense against these pervasive risks.

Importantly, cultivating digital literacy must transcend individual effort, embedding itself in educational curricula across disciplines. Integrating lesson plans that combine hands-on social media projects with critical analysis activities fosters these competencies from an early age. Interdisciplinary approaches—merging literacy, technology, ethics, and communication studies—prepare learners to engage thoughtfully with the digital world as informed citizens. For example, assignments encouraging students to evaluate the credibility of news articles, create multimedia presentations, or simulate online community management harness experiential learning to solidify abstract concepts.

The constellation of digital literacy competencies coalesces into a framework for equitable, ethical, and effective social media engagement. Users equipped with critical evaluation skills, algorithmic awareness, privacy management, respectful communication, creative expression, data interpretation, cybersecurity savvy, and curricular support are better positioned to navigate the complex digital landscape confidently. This holistic proficiency transforms social media from a chaotic expanse into a space of informed dialogue, innovation, and connection—qualities essential for thriving in the 21st-century information age.

Chapter 6

Social Media and Politics

This chapter examines the profound intersections between social media and political life. We begin by exploring how digital platforms enable grassroots activism and mobilization, then analyze how politicians harness these tools for campaigning and voter outreach. Building on that, we investigate the shaping of public opinion through framing, influencers, and algorithmic dynamics. We then confront the threats of election interference and manipulation, survey regulatory and policy responses, and conclude with in-depth case studies that distill lessons and anticipate future trends.

6.1 Online Activism and Social Movements

Digital activism refers to the use of the internet and social media platforms for political engagement, social advocacy, and collective action. Unlike traditional protest methods—marches, sit-ins, or printed pamphlets—digital activism unfolds in virtual spaces where actions such as sharing information, signing petitions, or coordinating events happen with unprecedented speed and reach. This form of activism is not a wholesale replacement of street-level activism but a powerful complement, expanding the ways people organize and express dissent beyond physical boundaries.

The roots of online activism stretch back to simpler digital tools, long before the era of Twitter and Instagram. Early internet activists relied on listservs and email petitions to rally support around causes. These text-based mailing lists created virtual communities for discussion and action, albeit limited in scale and immediacy. As social media platforms emerged, the capacity for rapid dissemination and user-generated content revolutionized movement-building. Hashtag campaigns, starting in the late 2000s, became a defining innovation—organizing scattered voices around a shared label that could trend globally, drawing attention and solidarity with minimal friction.

Hashtags embody this viral mobilization. Consider the #ArabSpring, a series of uprisings across the Middle East beginning in 2010, where social media became both a tool for real-time documentation and a catalyst for coordination. Activists used hashtags to share images, videos, and reports that bypassed state-controlled media, drawing international scrutiny and encouraging mass participation. Similarly, #BlackLivesMatter, first tweeted in 2013, transformed from a phrase into a dynamic, decentralized movement confronting systemic racial injustice. The hashtag allowed dispersed advocates worldwide to connect their local struggles with a broader narrative, amplifying voices that might otherwise be marginalized.

Central to these successes is the concept of networked decentralization. Unlike traditional hierarchies dependent on charismatic leaders or formal structures, digital movements often operate as leaderless collectives. This peer-to-peer coordination enables rapid scaling, resilience against targeted repression, and adaptation to shifting political landscapes. Each participant can contribute independently, creating a patchwork of initiatives that reinforce one another without a single command center. This fluid organization challenges conventional notions of activism by privileging agility and distributed ownership over rigid protocol.

Social media platforms amplify these decentralized dynamics by providing organizers with versatile tools. Event pages on Facebook allow straightforward mobilization, live video streams create immediacy and emotional impact, while group chats facilitate discreet planning and rapid response. Twitter's real-time feed enables participants to follow developments as they unfold and to broadcast calls to action instantly. These affordances turn users into not just consumers of information but active agents in shaping and sharing the movement's narrative.

Online spaces also serve as hubs for resource mobilization. Crowdfunding campaigns can quickly gather financial support from a dispersed base, democratizing fundraising beyond traditional gatekeepers. Volunteer recruitment through social media invites wider participation by breaking geographical and social barriers. The ease of disseminating educational materials, legislative updates, or instructions for protest tactics empowers individuals with knowledge often withheld or obscured by mainstream sources. These capacities underscore how digital platforms extend activism into tangible, practical realms.

Crucially, online activism often does not remain confined to the screen. Digital campaigns have consistently led to offline actions—street protests, town hall meetings, and policy lobbying. Moments like the Women's March in 2017 demonstrated how online organizing could culminate in massive physical gatherings, uniting millions around a shared cause. Digital announcements, maps, and safety guidelines have likewise enhanced the effectiveness and safety of street demonstrations. This online-to-offline translation refutes early critiques that internet-based activism is purely symbolic or disconnected from real-world change.

Nonetheless, the rise of what is sometimes called "slacktivism" presents a nuanced challenge. Low-effort acts—clicking "like," sharing a post, or changing a profile picture—may create a sense of participation without demanding deeper commitment. While such gestures can raise awareness and reduce barriers to entry, they risk diluting transformative potential if not accompanied by sustained, substantive engagement. Effective movements often blend accessible entry points with pathways for continued involvement, nurturing broader commitment over time.

Assessing the impact of online activism involves multiple metrics. Reach quantifies how broadly a message circulates across social networks. Engagement measures interactions such as comments, shares, and replies, indicating the depth of interest. More concrete indicators include petition signatures, fundraising totals, and attendance at coordinated events. While these numbers provide useful benchmarks, they cannot fully capture the multifaceted nature of political influence or cultural shifts that result from online activism. Nevertheless, they serve as valuable tools for organizers seeking to refine strategies and demonstrate success.

Together, these elements illustrate how social media has transformed collective action by reshaping the mechanisms of organizing, advocacy, and movement-building. Digital platforms enable expansive participation, rapid coordination, and innovative resource mobilization, challenging traditional power structures and amplifying marginalized voices. While not without limitations and new pitfalls, online activism represents a significant evolution in political engagement—a dynamic interplay between virtual networks and real-world change that continues to shape the future of social movements.

6.2 Politicians and Campaigning on Social Media

The landscape of political campaigning has undergone a profound transformation in the digital age, pivoting away from traditional broadcast advertisements toward increasingly sophisticated and targeted outreach on social media platforms. This shift reflects broader changes in media consumption habits and the opportunities offered by digital technologies to engage voters directly and intimately. No longer confined to thirty-second TV spots or mass mailings, political actors now inhabit a space where every tweet, post, or livestream can be a carefully calibrated element of a broader communication strategy.

Central to this modern approach is the crafting of a compelling candidate brand and an authentic, yet strategically curated, online persona. Politicians use social media not simply to broadcast messages, but to tell stories about themselves that resonate emotionally and ideologically with diverse audiences. Through a mix of polished videos, candid behind-the-scenes glimpses, and interactive live sessions, candidates build narratives that emphasize consistency, relatability, and values alignment. This branding acts as a digital

147

handshake, revealing character and priorities while inviting followers into a seemingly personal relationship that traditional media engagements could never achieve.

Underpinning these branded personas is the power of data-driven microtargeting, a game-changer in political outreach. Campaigns harness vast troves of voter data, from demographics to online behavior, and segment their audiences with remarkable precision. Tailored messages are then crafted to appeal to the specific concerns, hopes, or fears of each subgroup—whether young urban voters, rural conservatives, or swing voters in battleground districts. This surgical precision maximizes the impact of each post or ad, increasing the likelihood of persuasion or mobilization far beyond the blunt instruments of blanket advertising.

The stories these campaigns tell online are rarely random—they are embedded within carefully designed narrative frameworks and content strategies. Storytelling becomes a vehicle not just for information, but for framing policy stances, humanizing complex issues, and eliciting emotional responses. A post about healthcare reform might highlight a working mother's struggles, while climate policy is illustrated through vivid imagery of natural disasters. Emotional appeals—hope, fear, pride—are consciously calibrated to activate cognitive and affective channels in voters, engaging them in ways that raw policy details alone could not achieve. The digital environment, with its mix of text, images, and video, offers unparalleled versatility for these narrative experiments.

Engagement is no longer a one-way street either. Campaigns actively cultivate feedback loops, using real-time Q&A sessions, comment moderation, and personalized responses to foster a sense of dialogue and responsiveness. These interactions not only reinforce the candidate's image as accessible and attentive but also yield valuable insights into voter concerns and sentiment. Strategies such as "Ask Me Anything" events or Instagram Story polls turn passive followers into active participants, deepening investment in the campaign. Yet, this responsiveness carries risks—it demands constant vigilance to manage misinformation, trolling, or inappropriate comments, requiring dedicated teams and nuanced digital diplomacy.

Fundraising strategies have likewise evolved, integrating seamlessly into social media ecosystems. Digital platforms enable campaigns to mobilize small donors en masse, often through viral peer-to-peer fundraising drives where supporters are empowered to solicit contributions within their personal networks. Automated appeals leverage data to time donation requests just right—after a stirring speech or in response to breaking news—while offering convenient one-click payment options. This democratization of fundraising has not only broadened the donor base but also introduced new dynamics of speed and scale, allowing campaigns to sustain momentum and respond swiftly to financial needs.

In the fast-moving world of social media, rapid response and crisis management are critical. Political teams utilize hashtags, coordinated posting schedules, and targeted messaging to counter controversies, debunk false claims, or shift the narrative before stories gain traction. Speed is of the essence; a well-placed tweet or video can neutralize damage or even transform crises into opportunities for demonstrating leadership under pressure. These digital countermeasures are continuous and multifaceted, blending public relations, social listening, and content creation in real-time to safeguard reputations.

Promotion on social media unfolds across a spectrum

149

from organic to paid approaches. Volunteer-driven outreach amplifies messages through shares, retweets, and grassroots mobilization, often appearing more authentic and trustworthy. In contrast, sponsored advertising campaigns offer precise control over reach and frequency, ensuring that key messages penetrate targeted demographics. Successful campaigns adeptly blend both, nurturing a core of enthusiastic supporters who generate organic buzz, while strategically investing in paid ads to fill gaps, test messaging, or reach reluctant audiences.

However, this digital terrain is fraught with challenges related to transparency and ethics. Practices such as dark ads—targeted messages hidden from broader public scrutiny—raise questions about accountability and fairness. Issues of data privacy loom large, as campaigns rely on extensive personal information often gathered through opaque means. Moreover, inconsistent disclosure requirements for online political advertising have sparked debates over how to preserve the democratic ideal of informed electorates. Navigating these complexities requires not only compliance with evolving regulations but also a commitment to ethical campaigning that respects voter autonomy and trust.

Drawing these threads together, modern digital campaigning encapsulates a blend of innovative technology, narrative craftsmanship, and community-building. Effective politicking on social media demands agility, both in messaging and in reaction, as well as a nuanced understanding of audience segmentation and emotional resonance. Yet, it also presents pitfalls— from overreliance on data analytics that may neglect grassroots authenticity, to ethical dilemmas that can erode public confidence. For political actors, mastering social media is no longer optional but essential, a dynamic arena where the art and science of persuasion converge and where the shape of electoral contests is increasingly decided.

6.3 Shaping Public Opinion

In the sprawling digital agora of today's social media platforms, public opinion is far from a spontaneous crowd consensus; it is meticulously sculpted by a constellation of forces working in tandem. Algorithms, influencers, and the intricate dynamics of networked communities combine to steer what people see, how they interpret information, and ultimately, what they believe. Understanding this subtle choreography reveals how agenda-setting, framing, and polarization emerge not just organically but as outcomes of technological design and social behavior.

At the heart of agenda-setting are the algorithms that decide which topics trend and which voices are amplified. Platforms curate "trending" features and promoted content to highlight specific issues, effectively prioritizing what users should care about. This is no simple reflection of public interest but a calculated sequencing: by clustering and elevating certain posts, these systems create a shared focal point—be it a viral news story, a political slogan, or a social cause. The result is a digital spotlight that guides collective attention, often shaping it before individual opinions are fully formed.

But what gets spotlighted is only part of the story. The way issues are presented—how they are framed— exerts a powerful influence on perception. Framing operates through selective language, vivid imagery, and the strategic use of hashtags that tap into cultural undercurrents. For example, a protest might be

151

framed as a "movement for justice" or a "disruptive riot," shaping attitudes toward participants and their goals. Hashtags such as #BlackLivesMatter or #FakeNews perform more than categorization; they embed narratives and invite users to take sides. This narrative construction is a key tool in molding public discourse, turning abstract issues into emotionally charged stories that resonate with or repel specific audiences.

Central to this process are influencers and opinion leaders, users with outsized reach and credibility within their networks. Their endorsements or criticisms can sway beliefs and mobilize followers extensively. Unlike traditional media gatekeepers, these high-profile users often blend personal authenticity with persuasive messaging, creating a potent fusion of storytelling and advocacy. When an influencer champions a cause, endorses a candidate, or shares a hot take, their followers are not mere passive recipients but active participants who amplify these signals further, often without critical scrutiny.

The mechanics of persuasion on social media have also adapted to the digital vernacular of memes and short videos. Memetic persuasion encapsulates complex political ideas into shareable, digestible formats that ripple rapidly through networks. A meme's humor or simplicity masks sophisticated techniques of framing and emotional appeal, enabling swift transmission of political identities and ideologies. Political memes can ridicule opponents, celebrate heroes, or highlight grievances, all in a few seconds of scrolling time. This packaging of ideas caters to contemporary attention spans and creates viral cascades that both reflect and shape public sentiment.

Emotions provide the fuel that powers this engine

of sharing. Content that evokes strong feelings—whether anger, hope, fear, or outrage—is more likely to be disseminated widely. Anger can drive a sense of urgency and mobilization, while hope can inspire collective action. Fear often triggers defensive responses, pushing users into their ideological corners. This emotional contagion amplifies content dissemination and, at times, provokes heightened polarization as users rally around emotionally charged narratives rather than measured debate.

Algorithmic amplification deepens these effects by reinforcing content that generates engagement. Recommendation systems measure users' clicks, likes, shares, and dwell time, promoting posts that trigger intense reactions. As a result, content that confirms preexisting beliefs or incites strong emotional responses is systematically boosted, increasing its visibility and influence. This feedback loop not only intensifies the volume of certain viewpoints but also marginalizes less sensational or nuanced perspectives, shaping the boundaries of public discourse.

This amplification contributes directly to the formation of echo chambers and filter bubbles—digital environments where users are primarily exposed to information and opinions that mirror their own. Personalization algorithms craft feeds tailored to individual preferences, often at the expense of ideological diversity. Over time, this selective exposure reinforces existing beliefs, reducing opportunities for encountering challenging or contradictory viewpoints. The network effect further entrenches these bubbles as users connect predominantly with like-minded peers, fostering homogeneity and deepening polarization.

Recognizing these risks, platforms and researchers have experimented with interventions aimed at broadening

153

exposure and mitigating division. Some employ prompts encouraging users to consider alternative viewpoints, while others integrate cross-ideological content subtly into feeds to spark curiosity without alienation. Additionally, giving users greater control over algorithmic curation—such as adjustable filters or transparent explanation of why content appears— empowers more mindful consumption. Although complex and contested, these efforts reflect a growing awareness that diversity in information diets is crucial for healthy public discourse.

Beyond shaping what content circulates, new tools like sentiment analysis and social listening enable detailed measurement of public mood and discourse trends at scale. By parsing millions of posts, these technologies detect shifts in emotional tone, emerging concerns, and dominant narratives. Public officials, marketers, and scholars use these insights to gauge collective responses in real time, informing communication strategies and policymaking. Sentiment analysis thus serves as a digital thermometer of societal temperature, sensitizing stakeholders to the evolving opinions that shape democratic processes.

Taken together, these forces illustrate how social media accelerates the dynamics of public opinion while simultaneously fragmenting its landscape. Agenda-setting through trending topics channels collective attention; framing constructs competing narratives; influencers mobilize communities; emotional drivers spur viral sharing; and algorithms systematically amplify certain content while enclosing users within echo chambers. This interplay generates a rapid, complex, and often polarized discourse environment, where opinions are shaped less by direct deliberation and more by the architecture of digital influence.

The challenge lies in understanding and navigating this complex terrain—not only to recognize the mechanisms shaping public opinion but to foster a more informed, diverse, and resilient democratic conversation. As social media continues to evolve, so too must our approaches to engaging with it critically, ensuring it serves as a platform for connection rather than division.

6.4 Election Interference and Manipulation

Elections, once confined to physical ballot boxes and town halls, have increasingly migrated into the digital domain, where new vulnerabilities and tactics have emerged to manipulate outcomes and undermine trust. The online environment offers a potent toolkit for actors—ranging from foreign governments to private interest groups—to subtly or overtly interfere with electoral processes. The integrity of democracy hinges not only on safeguarding voting mechanics but also on protecting the informational ecosystem in which voters form their decisions. Understanding the multifaceted nature of online election interference requires disentangling an array of tactics, technologies, and vulnerabilities that coalesce to distort public perception and political debate.

At the heart of this phenomenon are various forms of online interference that blur the lines between covert influence and overt disinformation. Covert influence campaigns often involve clandestine operations designed to steer public opinion without revealing their origin, employing fake personas, deceptive messaging, and hidden sponsorships. Overt disinformation, by contrast, involves openly false or misleading content deliberately crafted to sow confusion, distrust, or polarization. These tactics are not isolated but deployed interactively; for example, an overtly false news story may be initially seeded for viral spread through covert bot networks or troll farms operating behind the scenes.

Prominent examples bring these abstract threats into sharp relief. The 2016 United States presidential election became a watershed moment, exposing how foreign actors exploited social media platforms to influence voter attitudes. Russian-backed entities orchestrated a sophisticated campaign using fake accounts, divisive memes, and targeted advertisements to amplify societal fractures—around race, immigration, and political identity—at an unprecedented scale. Similarly, the Brexit referendum in the United Kingdom witnessed coordinated online efforts to sway public opinion through misleading narratives and aggressively spreading misinformation, further igniting debates about the ethical and geopolitical implications of digital influence.

Central to these operations are bot networks—automated or semi-automated accounts programmed to mimic real users. These bots can inflate the visibility of a particular message by generating likes, shares, and comments, creating the illusion of widespread support or concern. By systematically drowning out opposing voices and flooding timelines with repetitive content, bot networks shape online discourse, manipulate trending topics, and manufacture consensus where none exists. Their sophistication varies, with some trivially automated while others employ machine learning techniques to engage in more convincing interactions, making detection increasingly challenging.

Complementing bots are coordinated troll operations—groups, sometimes state-sponsored, tasked with sowing discord through incendiary, polarizing content.

These trolls exploit cultural fault lines by amplifying grievances, spreading conspiracy theories, and attacking political opponents. Unlike bots, they rely on human creativity and adaptability, adjusting tactics in real time to evade platform moderation. The sheer scale and professional organization of some operations reveal an alarming degree of coordination aimed at undermining democratic debate from within.

An equally potent weapon in the election interference arsenal is data harvesting, whereby vast troves of personal information are collected—often without explicit consent—and analyzed to create detailed voter profiles. Such data enables microtargeting: delivering bespoke advertisements and propaganda tailored to individual psychological traits, political predispositions, or social networks. These precision-targeted messages can exploit fears, biases, or aspirations with surgical accuracy, steering voters toward desired behaviors or discouraging participation altogether. The Cambridge Analytica scandal exemplifies the risks that arise when data and psychology intersect with political campaigns, highlighting ethical dilemmas and privacy concerns inherent in digital elections.

Emerging technologies compound these threats in insidious ways. Perhaps the most unsettling among them are deepfakes—AI-generated videos or audio clips that fabricate convincingly realistic but entirely false impressions of individuals saying or doing things they never did. Such synthetic media can erode trust in authentic communications, blur truth and fiction, and provide ready-made "evidence" to discredit opponents or ignite conflicts. As deepfake technology matures, combating its malicious use becomes a race between detection tools and increasingly sophisticated forgeries.

Underlying all these tactics are platform vulnerabilities

and security gaps ripe for exploitation. Social media algorithms, designed to maximize engagement, often inadvertently amplify sensationalist or divisive content. Weak verification systems allow fake accounts to proliferate at scale, while inconsistent moderation policies create patchy enforcement landscapes across platforms and regions. In some cases, political advertising rules are vague or poorly implemented online, enabling stealth campaigns to operate with impunity. These technical and institutional weaknesses create fertile ground for manipulators to flourish.

Recognizing the complexity of these challenges, technology companies, researchers, and civil society organizations have developed a range of detection and mitigation strategies. Fact-checking partnerships work to rapidly identify and label false claims, providing users with context and corrections. Sophisticated bot detection algorithms analyze behavioral patterns and network characteristics to flag suspicious accounts. User alerts and educational campaigns aim to build "digital literacy," empowering voters to recognize and resist manipulative content. While none of these solutions is foolproof, combined efforts help raise the cost and reduce the effectiveness of interference attempts.

Beyond technological remedies, legal and regulatory countermeasures play a vital role. Governments and international bodies are crafting laws to increase transparency in political advertising, impose sanctions on malicious foreign actors, and facilitate cross-border information sharing on interference tactics. Collaborative efforts such as dedicated cybersecurity task forces and joint investigations reflect an acknowledgment that election interference transcends national boundaries, requiring coordinated responses. Balancing these interventions with protections for free speech and privacy remains an evolving legal tightrope.

Taken together, these evolving tactics constitute a dynamic and multifaceted threat to electoral integrity. The interplay between covert influence campaigns, automated amplification, human-operated troll networks, and sophisticated data-driven targeting forms a complex ecosystem designed to manipulate, distract, and divide. As digital technology reshapes the political landscape, safeguarding elections demands constant vigilance, technological innovation, and societal awareness. Only by appreciating the depth and breadth of online election interference can democratic societies hope to defend the foundational principle that every vote counts—and counts for something real.

6.5 Regulation and Public Policy

The governance of political content online presents a persistent and intricate challenge: how to safeguard open discourse while preventing the spread of harmful abuse, disinformation, and manipulation. The internet, once hailed as a democratic space for free exchange, has become a battleground where the boundaries between expression and harm blur. Regulation and public policy efforts seek to navigate this tension, balancing the fundamental right to free speech with the equally urgent need to protect individuals and society from damaging content.

At the heart of this balancing act lies the question: how much control should platforms exert over political speech? On one side stands the ideal of an unfiltered marketplace of ideas, echoing classical liberal values. On the other, the reality of coordinated misinformation campaigns, hate speech, harassment, and even threats to electoral integrity demand intervention. The challenge is compounded by the scale and velocity of online communication, which far exceed traditional media's reach and control mechanisms.

To address these concerns, many platforms have adopted forms of self-regulation, crafting community standards that delineate acceptable behavior and content. These standards often prohibit hate speech, incitement to violence, and coordinated harmful activity. Yet enforcement is inherently complex and controversial. Transparency reporting has emerged as a key tool, with platforms disclosing metrics about content removals, policy enforcement, and governmental requests. Ad-archive tools, which catalog political advertisements and their sponsors, provide an unprecedented window into online political campaigning. Such measures exemplify a cautious attempt by platforms to demonstrate accountability while preserving operational autonomy.

However, self-regulation alone has not quelled calls for more robust oversight. Governments and public institutions increasingly intervene with legal frameworks tailored to digital realities. In the United States, Section 230 of the Communications Decency Act famously shields platforms from liability for user-generated content, underpinning the modern internet ecosystem. Yet this immunity is under scrutiny, with critics arguing it encourages lax moderation or fuels harmful content propagation. Conversely, the European Union's General Data Protection Regulation (GDPR) pioneers user privacy and data protection, influencing political content dynamics by regulating targeting and personal data use. The EU's Digital Services Act now aims to hold platforms accountable for systemic risks, including disinformation and illegal content, signaling a shift toward more assertive governance.

Integral to these debates is the concept of intermediary liability and immunity. Should platforms be treated merely as passive conduits for information, or as active gatekeepers responsible for the content they host? This question shapes the contours of regulatory proposals worldwide. Immunity shields platforms from being sued over user posts but raises the risk of abdicated responsibility. Strengthened liability, by contrast, could incentivize over-censorship or stifle innovation. The middle ground—conditional immunity tied to good-faith content moderation—sparks nuanced discussions about accountability and free expression.

Transparency and disclosure mandates increasingly underpin regulatory efforts. Political ads are subject to requirements such as sponsor labeling, spending disclosures, and the archiving of ad content in publicly accessible databases. These policies respond to the opaque nature of online political influence, seeking to illuminate who is funding campaigns and how voters are targeted. Algorithmic audits—reviews of recommendation engines and content-ranking systems—are proposed or implemented to reveal biases and prevent amplification of harmful political content. Such measures aim to shift platforms from black-box arbiters to accountable participants in democratic processes.

Regulation also targets electoral compliance and finance rules to combat foreign interference and illicit campaign contributions. Jurisdictions implement restrictions on political advertising by foreign entities and monitor sophisticated voter-targeting tactics enabled by big data. These laws strive to ensure that elections are fair and transparent, preventing malign actors from exploiting digital platforms to undermine democratic legitimacy. However, enforcement remains complicated by jurisdictional boundaries and technological complexity.

Effective governance often calls for multi-stakeholder collaboration, where governments, platforms, civil society, academics, and user communities jointly navigate policy formulation and enforcement. This pluralistic approach recognizes that no single actor can impose comprehensive solutions. Collective action forums foster dialogue, share expertise, and help balance competing values—free expression, privacy, fairness, and security—in complex digital ecosystems.

Comparing global regulatory approaches reveals stark differences shaped by cultural, legal, and political contexts. The European Union favors proactive, rights-based regulation with robust privacy protections and platform accountability. The United States emphasizes free speech and innovation, favoring lighter government intervention but rigorous debates over Section 230's scope. Countries like India pursue assertive content takedown mandates, sometimes criticized for censorship. Emerging economies face unique challenges, balancing political stability, free expression, and rapid digital expansion. These contrasts underscore the difficulty of crafting uniform global standards amid competing priorities.

Alongside formal legislation, industry codes of conduct represent voluntary commitments by platforms to adopt best practices around content moderation, transparency, and user protections. These codes, often developed in consultation with multiple stakeholders, provide flexible frameworks adaptable to fast-evolving digital challenges. While lacking legal enforceability, they serve as important complements to regulation, signaling platform willingness to act responsibly and maintain public trust.

The mosaic of policy approaches—self-regulation, government oversight, transparency mandates, stakeholder collaboration, and voluntary codes—reflects the multifaceted nature of regulating political content online. Each strategy brings strengths and limitations. Self-regulation offers agility but may lack consistency or accountability; legal mandates provide enforceability but risk overreach or rigidity; multi-stakeholder initiatives foster inclusivity but may slow decision-making. Balancing these approaches is essential for fostering a digital environment that supports vibrant, informed democratic discourse without becoming a breeding ground for abuse or manipulation.

Ultimately, the regulation of political content is an ongoing negotiation, one that must adapt to technological innovation, shifting political landscapes, and evolving societal norms. The path forward lies not in simplistic cures but in layered, nuanced policies that respect free expression while mitigating harms, empower users while holding platforms accountable, and engage multiple voices in shaping the digital public square.

6.6 Case Studies in Social Media Politics

The transformative power of social media in politics is best understood through landmark moments where digital platforms have both shaped and reflected political currents. These case studies reveal complex interactions between technology, human agency, and socio-political structures, illuminating the strategies activists, politicians, and regimes employ—and their far-reaching consequences.

163

The **Arab Spring (2010–11)** stands as a seminal example of networked coordination catalyzing mass mobilization. Across Tunisia, Egypt, and beyond, digital tools like Facebook and Twitter enabled activists to share information rapidly, organize protests, and circumvent state-controlled media. These platforms functioned not merely as communication channels but as digital public squares where narratives of resistance and hope circulated. The decentralized nature of this mobilization proved difficult for authoritarian regimes to suppress quickly; however, they responded with internet blackouts, cyber-surveillance, and propaganda. This interplay highlighted the dual-edged nature of social media—it can empower grassroots movements but also provoke sophisticated authoritarian countermeasures. Importantly, the Arab Spring demonstrated how the immediacy and network effects of social media amplify collective action, albeit within contested political environments.

Moving to a different political context, the **2016 U.S. Presidential Election** exemplifies a more adversarial and strategic use of social media grounded in data-driven targeting and disinformation. Here, digital platforms became arenas for both domestic campaigning and foreign interference. Sophisticated algorithmic profiling allowed campaigns and external actors to micro-target voters with tailored messages, often exploiting social divisions. The deployment of bots, fake accounts, and misinformation campaigns underscored vulnerabilities intrinsic to digital ecosystems. Platforms reacted post-facto with content moderation efforts, fact-checking, and transparency initiatives, but this response often lagged behind the pace of manipulation. The election revealed that the power of social media could be mobilized not only for participatory democracy but also for undermining it, raising urgent questions about platform governance and electoral security.

In contrast, the **#MeToo Movement** showcased social media as a tool for viral testimonies and solidarity that spurred profound cultural and policy shifts. Originating from grassroots disclosures of sexual harassment, the widespread adoption of the #MeToo hashtag created collective visibility for previously marginalized voices. The movement's momentum was propelled by the ease with which individuals could publicize personal experiences, thereby transforming isolated incidents into a shared public reckoning. This digital solidarity transcended borders and professions, compelling institutions to reconsider harassment policies and power dynamics. The case illustrates social media's unique capacity to personalize politics and mobilize empathy at scale, translating virtual expressions into tangible social change.

Similarly, the **#FridaysForFuture** climate strikes, driven by youth leadership and global influencers like Greta Thunberg, underline how social media facilitates sustained, transnational activism. The movement's digital footprint enabled synchronization of local climate protests worldwide, channeling youthful frustration into coordinated political pressure. Influencer support amplified outreach exponentially, while strategic use of hashtags maintained visibility in crowded digital spaces. This case highlights how social media can nurture ongoing engagement rather than momentary spikes, linking individual agency with global environmental politics and demonstrating the evolving scope of digital activism.

Case	Year	Digital Tactic	Political Outcome
Arab Spring	2010–11	Networked coordination, real-time updates	Toppled regimes, mixed democratic transitions
2016 U.S. Election	2016	Data-driven targeting, disinformation	Electoral disruption, regulatory debates
#MeToo Movement	2017–present	Viral testimonies, solidarity hashtags	Policy reforms, cultural shifts
#FridaysForFuture	2018–present	Global mobilization, influencer amplification	Heightened climate awareness, policy engagement

Table 6.1: Summary of Key Social Media Political Case Studies

Comparing these cases reveals persistent themes and divergent outcomes. Success often hinges on balancing spontaneity with organization, authenticity with strategy, and openness with resilience against manipulation. For instance, the Arab Spring's decentralized nature enabled rapid mobilization but lacked institutional follow-through, while the #MeToo Movement combined personal narratives with sustained advocacy, yielding deeper structural impact. The 2016 U.S. election underscores how digital tactics can be weaponized to erode trust, posing vulnerabilities absent in earlier, predominantly grassroots movements like #FridaysForFuture, which capitalized on positive influencer dynamics and clear messaging.

These contrasting trajectories offer insight into the evolving relationship between social media and political agency. Platforms that foster horizontal, networked action are powerful but also fragile in the face of disinformation and surveillance. Moreover, the scope of digital activism has broadened—from overthrowing regimes to reshaping cultural norms and focusing global attention on issues like climate change. The lessons unequivocally suggest that social media is neither a panacea nor a mere adjunct to politics but a contested terrain where power, ideology, and technology intersect dynamically.

Looking ahead, emerging trends present both opportunities and challenges. Advances in artificial intelligence promise more personalized and immersive political engagement but could also exacerbate echo chambers, manipulate sentiment, and automate misinformation. Decentralized platforms based on blockchain technology promise greater control and censorship resistance but raise questions about governance and inclusivity. Simultaneously, evolving regulations—ranging from content moderation to data privacy—will shape how digital politics unfolds and who governs these virtual commons.

For practitioners navigating this landscape, several actionable insights emerge. Activists should invest in building resilient, adaptable networks that combine online and offline tactics. Policymakers must pursue nuanced frameworks promoting transparency and accountability without stifling expression. Campaigners benefit from ethical data practices and cultivating trust beyond micro-targeting gimmicks. Crucially, all actors should remain vigilant about the vulnerabilities inherent to digital media ecosystems, from algorithmic biases to coordinated manipulation efforts.

Ultimately, these case studies exemplify how social media has reshaped contemporary politics by accelerating communication, amplifying marginalized voices, and fostering global solidarity, while simultaneously introducing novel risks of fragmentation and control.

Understanding these dynamics demands an ongoing appreciation of technology as both an enabler and obstacle in the political arena. The digital public sphere is neither utopian nor dystopian but a site of continuous negotiation, requiring informed engagement to harness its promise and mitigate its pitfalls.

Chapter 7

Business, Marketing, and the Digital Economy

This chapter examines how social media drives modern commerce, from targeted advertising and influencer partnerships to brand reputation management and direct e-commerce. We explore customer engagement and support dynamics, and conclude by highlighting entrepreneurial opportunities within the creator and gig economies. Each section builds on core concepts to reveal how businesses leverage social platforms for growth and innovation.

7.1 Advertising on Social Media

The remarkable shift from traditional mass-market advertising to targeted social media campaigns represents one of the most transformative stories in marketing history. Where once brands relied on billboards, newspapers, and television spots to reach broad audiences, the advent of digital technology and its integration with social platforms has revolutionized the art of persuasion. No longer must advertisers cast a wide net and hope for serendipity; instead, sophisticated data-driven strategies enable them to zoom in on individuals with pinpoint precision, tailoring messages to resonate deeply with distinct segments. This evolution mirrors broader societal changes—the rise of mobile devices, instantaneous connectivity, and vast troves of user data—as social media platforms have emerged not just as communication tools but as highly effective marketplaces for attention.

At the heart of social advertising lies the concept of *audience targeting*. It begins with demographic filters—age, gender, location—laying a simple foundation for reaching groups that share obvious traits. But targeting soon becomes more intricate by incorporating interest-based segmentation, harnessing users' likes, follows, and online behavior to define groups who share passions, hobbies, or purchasing intent. More recently, *look-alike audiences* offer an ingenious method: advertisers seed a campaign with a source audience—say, loyal customers—and the platform's algorithms identify new individuals whose profiles and behaviors closely match that seed. This expands reach intelligently, blending existing customer insights with machine learning to discover potential buyers who might otherwise have remained invisible to traditional methods.

Understanding the various *ad formats* is equally critical for crafting compelling social media campaigns. The humble image ad, essentially a single photo coupled with text, remains a staple for grabbing attention with visual storytelling. Yet, video ads have surged as the medium of choice, delivering dynamic narratives and emotional energy in mere seconds. Carousel ads invite users to swipe through multiple images or videos, encouraging exploration and demonstrating product variety. Story ads exploit the ephemeral, full-screen vertical format popularized by Snapchat and Instagram, creating immersive experiences that disappear within 24 hours—perfect for urgency or seasonal promotions. Sponsored content, meanwhile, often masquerades as organic posts from influencers or brands the audience already follows, blending authenticity with subtle persuasion. Together, these formats offer advertisers a rich palette to align creative strategy with campaign goals.

Navigating the advertising interfaces of major platforms requires both agility and an understanding of distinct ecosystems. Facebook's Ad Manager is a powerhouse, providing a robust yet complex dashboard enabling fine-grained control over targeting, bidding, and creative assets; its integration with Instagram through the same interface simplifies cross-posting campaigns. Instagram emphasizes visual appeal and user engagement, offering a sleek interface designed for mobile-first ad creation, focusing on stories and reels. LinkedIn, by contrast, caters to a professional audience and features tools optimized for B2B advertising, with targeting options centered on job titles, industries, and company size—ideal for recruiters or enterprise software vendors. Twitter's ad platform centers on real-time engagement and conversation, providing unique opportunities to capitalize on trending topics, hashtags, and timely events. Each platform's distinctive approach shapes how advertisers craft and deploy campaigns, emphasizing different user behaviors and expectations.

Budgeting and bidding strategies form the financial backbone of social media advertising. Advertisers can choose among several pricing models: *CPM* (cost per mille) charges for every thousand impressions served, optimal for brand awareness; *CPC* (cost per click) charges only when users click the ad, focusing on direct engagement; and *CPA* (cost per acquisition)

charges exclusively when a specified action, such as
a purchase or signup, occurs, aligning tightly with
conversion goals. Managing bids can be manual, where
advertisers set maximum amounts they are willing to
pay, or automated, where machine learning algorithms
optimize bidding in real time to achieve campaign
objectives efficiently. This blend of human control and
algorithmic assistance reflects the broader interplay
of strategy and technology in contemporary digital
marketing.

Key performance metrics translate campaign performance into actionable insights, guiding how advertisers
adjust strategies. *Impressions* count how many times an
ad is displayed, while *reach* measures the number of
unique individuals who see it—vital for understanding
penetration versus frequency.   The *click-through rate*
(CTR) reveals what percentage of viewers are motivated
to engage by clicking, serving as a proxy for relevance
and creative effectiveness. Most critically, the *cost per
acquisition* (CPA) quantifies how much an advertiser
spends to obtain a conversion, directly connecting
budget with return on investment.   Together, these
metrics form a diagnostic toolbox, enabling continuous
refinement and accountability.

Advertising on social media isn't a set-it-and-forget-it
endeavor; rather, it demands rigorous *A/B testing*—
controlled experiments where two or more versions of
an ad differ by just one variable such as headline, image,
or call to action. By comparing performance side-by-
side, advertisers learn what resonates best with their
audience. This iterative process extends beyond creative
elements to targeting parameters and scheduling,
revealing how even subtle changes can dramatically
alter effectiveness. In this way, A/B testing transforms
guesswork into evidence-based decisions, empowering

marketers to optimize campaigns dynamically rather than relying on intuition alone.

Underpinning much of this optimization is the growing role of *algorithmic ad delivery*. Social media platforms deploy machine learning algorithms that continuously analyze user behavior and campaign responses, adjusting ad placements and bid strategies in real time to better meet objectives such as clicks, conversions, or video views. This intelligent automation allows campaigns to be both scalable and precise, maximizing impact while managing costs. However, it also raises questions about transparency and control, as advertisers entrust decision-making to complex, proprietary systems—rendering the symbiosis between human strategy and machine intelligence a defining theme of modern advertising.

Despite these advances, social media advertising remains vulnerable to *ad fraud* and brand safety risks. Common fraud types include click fraud—where automated bots or malicious actors generate fake clicks, draining budgets without real engagement—and impression fraud, where ads are served invisibly or on low-quality sites. Brands must deploy verification tools and work closely with platforms to detect and mitigate such abuses. Brand safety also involves maintaining the integrity of where and how ads appear, avoiding placements alongside controversial or inappropriate content that could damage reputation. These challenges underscore the importance of vigilance and partnership in safeguarding both financial investment and public trust.

Successful social media campaigns follow a well-defined *lifecycle* from initial planning through execution, monitoring, and post-campaign analysis. Planning involves defining clear objectives, selecting target

audiences, crafting creatives, and establishing budgets.
Execution includes launching ads, managing bids, and
fine-tuning real-time delivery.   Monitoring leverages
dashboards and alerts to track key metrics, identify
issues, and capitalize on emerging opportunities.
Finally, post-campaign analysis examines outcomes
against goals, extracting lessons that inform future
strategies.   This cyclical process reflects a growing
professionalism and sophistication in social media
advertising, where data, creativity, and technology
interplay to create campaigns as dynamic and
multifaceted as the digital landscape itself.

7.2   Influencer Marketing

At its core, influencer marketing leverages the persuasive power of trusted individuals who resonate with
particular audiences, turning personal credibility into
a vehicle for brand communication. Unlike traditional
advertisements that rely on unilateral promotion,
influencer marketing thrives on relationships—
between creators and their followers, and between
brands and creators.   These influencers are not
merely spokespeople; they are content curators
and community builders who shape opinions and
spark conversations through authentic storytelling.
When an influencer shares a product, it is infused
with their personal endorsement, capturing attention
and encouraging genuine engagement that often
outperforms conventional ads.

Influencers are categorically distinguished by the
size and nature of their audiences, creating tiers
that correspond with different strategic uses. *Mega
influencers*—celebrities or public figures—boast
followings numbering in the millions, offering

unparalleled reach but sometimes at the cost of diminished engagement or perceived authenticity. *Macro influencers* often command hundreds of thousands of followers, striking a balance between wide visibility and niche relevance. *Micro influencers*, with follower counts in the tens of thousands, shine in delivering highly engaged, targeted communities, fostering trust that feels more intimate and less commercial. At the smallest scale, *nano influencers*, often everyday consumers with under ten thousand followers, provide hyper-localized, relatable endorsements, ideal for grassroots or hyper-specific campaigns. Each tier presents brands with distinct opportunities and challenges when amplifying messages.

Selecting the right influencer hinges on a nuanced assessment beyond mere follower numbers. Relevance to the brand and product category is paramount; an influencer who naturally embodies a brand's values and appeals to its target market stands a better chance of generating meaningful engagement. Authenticity is closely linked—followers can instinctively detect disingenuous endorsements, so an influencer's voice and content style must harmonize with the product's image. Audience fit involves demographic and psychographic alignment, ensuring the influencer's reach maps onto the desired consumer profile. Engagement rate, quantifiable through likes, comments, shares, and views, offers insight into how actively an influencer's audience interacts, often a stronger predictor of campaign success than raw follower counts. By weighing these criteria, brands mitigate the risk of a mismatch and enhance the likelihood of genuine amplification.

With influencer selection made, the partnership model defines the nature of collaboration, tailored to campaign goals and budgetary realities.

- **Gifting** represents the simplest form—brands provide free products hoping for organic promotion, a tactic best suited to products with strong intrinsic appeal or novelty.

- **Sponsored content** arrangements involve influencers creating posts explicitly compensated to feature the brand, often accompanied by specific messaging objectives and deadlines.

- **Affiliate marketing** models layer in performance incentives, granting influencers commissions for sales or clicks generated through their personalized links or promo codes, aligning remuneration with measurable results.

- The most strategic partnerships cultivate **long-term ambassadorships**, weaving the brand into the influencer's ongoing narrative and fostering a sense of shared identity that transcends episodic campaigns.

Each model carries unique dynamics, and the choice profoundly impacts authenticity, content quality, and audience reception.

Contractual details underpin effective influencer collaborations, clarifying expectations and safeguarding interests on both sides.

- Fee structures vary widely—from one-time flat rates to tiered payments dependent on deliverables or engagement thresholds.

- Performance incentives such as bonuses for hitting sales targets or virality milestones help motivate sustained effort and accountability.

176

- Some partnerships also embrace barter agreements, exchanging products or services for exposure, especially with smaller influencers or emerging creators.

- Contracts specify usage rights, content ownership, timelines, exclusivity clauses, and termination conditions, ensuring both brand consistency and creator freedom remain balanced.

Transparent and mutually agreeable terms lay the foundation for productive, frictionless campaigns.

Content co-creation marries brand objectives with influencer creativity, producing messages that resonate organically while adhering to strategic goals. The ideation process often involves collaborative brainstorming sessions where brand teams and creators align on key themes, tone, and campaign narratives. Influencers appreciate latitude to integrate their unique style and voice, as heavy-handed brand control can undermine authenticity and alienate followers. Approval workflows establish checkpoints to verify compliance with brand guidelines and legal requirements without stifling spontaneity. This dynamic exchange equips influencers to craft compelling narratives that feel both professional and personal, maximizing emotional connection and message clarity.

Navigating disclosure and compliance is critical in maintaining transparency and trust in influencer marketing. Regulatory bodies such as the Federal Trade Commission (FTC) in the United States mandate clear disclosures whenever content involves compensation or sponsorship, typically requiring hashtags like #ad or #sponsored to signal paid relationships. Platforms such as Instagram, YouTube, and TikTok have their own policies to ensure sponsored content is identifiable.

Failure to comply risks legal penalties and erosion
of consumer trust. Ethically, transparency fosters
long-term credibility for both brand and influencer,
reinforcing rather than eroding the authenticity that
underpins the entire marketing approach.

Evaluating the return on investment (ROI) in influencer
marketing demands both quantitative and qualitative
analyses.

- **Reach** quantifies the raw number of unique viewers exposed to the content.

- **Engagement rates** reveal how actively audiences
  interact through likes, comments, and shares.

- **Referral traffic** tracks how much audience activity
  flows from influencer content to brand websites or
  apps, often monitored with specialized UTM parameters or affiliate tracking tools.

- **Conversion attribution** connects downstream
  sales or sign-ups to the campaign, providing
  the clearest metric of financial impact, though
  challenges remain in isolating influencer effects
  from other marketing channels.

Analytical tools and dashboards increasingly harness artificial intelligence to paint a multi-dimensional picture
of campaign performance, enabling brands to optimize
and iterate more effectively.

Sustaining successful influencer collaborations extends
beyond a single campaign into long-term relationship
management. Authenticity deepens as brands and
influencers build rapport over time, often resulting in
more natural content and enthusiastic advocacy. Trust
nurtured through respectful communication and fair

compensation encourages influencers to prioritize the brand in their content ecosystem. Evolving campaign objectives might shift toward community building, product innovation partnerships, or co-branded ventures, reflecting a maturation of the relationship beyond transactional exchanges. Investing in these connections transforms influencers from marketing assets into brand allies, enriching both parties' value in an interconnected digital landscape.

Risk management remains an essential, if sometimes overlooked, dimension of influencer marketing. Brand reputation risks arise if influencers behave controversially, promote inappropriate content, or fail to properly disclose sponsored messages. Contractual safeguards such as morality clauses allow brands to terminate agreements if influencer conduct jeopardizes brand image. Conversely, creators must protect their intellectual property rights and creative freedom to avoid exploitation. Crisis communication plans prepare brands and influencers to respond swiftly and transparently to issues, preserving audience trust. Proactive vetting, ongoing monitoring, and open dialogue between brands and creators form frontline defenses, ensuring influencer marketing campaigns enhance rather than endanger brand equity.

Influencer marketing is far more than a passing trend; it reflects a fundamental shift in how brands communicate, harnessing social dynamics and personal influence. This nuanced dance of selection, collaboration, transparency, and measurement demands strategic finesse and genuine relationship-building. When done well, it unlocks powerful new avenues for authentic engagement and conversion in an increasingly fragmented media world.

7.3 Brand Reputation and Social Listening

In today's hyperconnected world, a brand's reputation is shaped as much by the marketplace as by myriad online conversations unfolding across social media, forums, blogs, and review sites. Monitoring these digital murmurs—an activity known as social listening—has evolved from mere curiosity into a strategic imperative. By tracking mentions and discerning sentiment, brands gain critical insight into public perception, enabling them to anticipate shifts, respond swiftly to reputational threats, and calibrate their messaging with finesse.

At its core, social listening involves collecting and analyzing references to a brand, its products, or related topics across various digital channels. The importance of this practice cannot be overstated: every comment, tweet, or post can reveal patterns in customer satisfaction, emerging trends, or brewing discontent. Companies that master social listening transform scattered data into a nuanced understanding of audience mood and preferences, which informs decisions ranging from marketing campaigns to product development.

The tools designed to aid this process vary in sophistication and scope. Platforms such as Brandwatch, Hootsuite, and native analytics tools each offer distinctive features tailored to different organizational needs. Brandwatch, for instance, excels in deep data mining and customizable dashboards, allowing users to drill down into demographics and sentiment with fine granularity. Hootsuite integrates social monitoring alongside publishing capabilities, facilitating real-time engagement while keeping an eye on trends across networks. Native analytics—such as Twitter Analytics or Facebook Insights—offer immediate but narrower views, focusing on platform-specific data rather than the wider digital ecosystem. Selecting the right tools often depends on balancing budget, desired depth, and agility, with many organizations opting for layered approaches that combine these resources.

At the heart of social listening is sentiment analysis—the art and science of classifying online mentions according to their emotional tone, be it positive, negative, or neutral. Automated techniques leverage natural language processing algorithms to scan large volumes of text, flagging phrases and keywords that suggest customer enthusiasm or frustration. Yet these systems, while impressive, are not infallible. Sarcasm, slang, and cultural nuances can elude purely algorithmic judgment, which is why many brands supplement automation with human moderation. A manual review layer ensures subtlety and context are captured, enabling more accurate interpretation of complex conversations. This hybrid approach helps brands not only quantify sentiment but understand its drivers and implications.

Early detection of trends and issues is another invaluable benefit of social listening. By continually analyzing data streams, brands can spot emerging topics before they coalesce into full-blown crises or viral campaigns. For example, a sudden spike in mentions involving a product flaw or a controversial advertisement may signal growing dissatisfaction. Identifying these signals promptly enables proactive intervention—whether through clarifying statements, targeted outreach, or even operational adjustments. This anticipatory vigilance saves reputations by turning potential disasters into manageable challenges.

When negative sentiment surges, real-time crisis monitoring and alerting systems come into play. Brands set thresholds calibrated to their typical mention

181

volumes and sentiment baselines, triggering immediate notifications when anomalies occur. These alerts empower rapid response teams to convene, assess the situation, and initiate carefully crafted communications to mitigate damage. The speed of detection and reaction often defines the boundary between a containable incident and a runaway public relations debacle.

Beyond detection, effective community management anchors social listening into a sustained dialogue with customers. Response protocols guide how teams engage with commenters—balancing transparency, empathy, and brand voice. Tone guidelines ensure replies are neither overly scripted nor off-brand; instead, they strive to humanize the organization while maintaining professionalism. Clear escalation paths channel complex issues from frontline social media managers to higher-level specialists, ensuring problems are addressed with appropriate authority and expertise. This structured yet personable approach fosters trust and loyalty, crucial ingredients in bolstering long-term reputation.

Insights gleaned from social listening feed back into strategic decision-making across the enterprise. Brands may refine messaging to emphasize values resonating with their audiences or modify products by addressing common complaints revealed through discussions. Policy shifts, whether in customer service protocols or corporate social responsibility initiatives, also often trace their origins to feedback harvested in the social sphere. This continuous loop turns reputation management from reactive firefighting into a dynamic process of adaptation and improvement.

Measuring reputation recovery after a crisis similarly requires a thoughtful framework. Brands track sentiment uplift—an improvement in positive mentions relative to prior downturns—and monitor share of voice, which compares a brand's presence to competitors within conversations. Changes in net promoter scores (NPS), reflecting customers' willingness to recommend the brand, provide further quantifiable evidence of reputational health. These metrics not only gauge recovery but signal areas needing continued attention.

Several key reputation metrics help contextualize social listening data:

- **Mention volume**: Captures raw activity—how many times a brand is referenced in a given period.

- **Engagement ratio**: Measures interactions—likes, shares, comments—in relation to volume, indicating how actively audiences respond.

- **Crisis duration**: Tracks the length of time negative sentiment dominates discourse, highlighting how protracted or contained incidents are.

Understanding the interplay of these metrics equips brands with a balanced view of reputation dynamics, avoiding overreactions to fleeting controversies or complacency in the face of lingering challenges.

Consider a real-world application: a global food company faced a viral social media outcry after a product recall linked to contamination. Social listening tools quickly detected an upsurge in negative mentions and hashtags spreading dissatisfaction. Automated sentiment flagged the spike, while human moderators identified the most influential voices driving the conversation. The company's crisis team activated instant alerts and deployed a carefully scripted response that acknowledged concerns, explained corrective measures, and offered compensation. Simultaneously, social media managers engaged users directly, answering questions and dispelling misinformation with transparency. Over the following weeks, sentiment analysis showed gradual improvement; share of voice returned to normal levels, and NPS surveys indicated regained customer confidence. This case underscores how tightly integrated social listening with community management mitigates reputational risks and paves the way to recovery.

Ultimately, brand reputation in the digital age demands vigilance and responsiveness grounded in robust social listening. It is a continuous conversation—ever evolving, rich with nuance, and fraught with challenges—that rewards those who listen attentively and act strategically. By harnessing a combination of technology, human insight, and measured engagement, brands transform the cacophony of online voices into a symphony of actionable knowledge, safeguarding their standing and fostering enduring connections with their audiences.

7.4   E-Commerce and Selling Online

The rapid rise of e-commerce has transformed the way individuals and businesses engage with consumers, enabling direct transactions within digital ecosystems that blur traditional retail boundaries. Platforms that once served primarily as social or entertainment hubs are now integrated marketplaces, offering seamless avenues for sellers to reach audiences without the friction of redirecting buyers to external sites. This fusion of content and commerce—known as social commerce—epitomizes a new paradigm, where shopping unfolds inside familiar apps rather than through isolated storefronts.

At its core, social commerce can be distinguished by two approaches. The first is *in-app shopping*, where purchases occur directly within the social platform, shortening the path from discovery to transaction. This experience is often supported by native product tags, embedded catalogs, and integrated payment systems. Conversely, platforms sometimes function as traffic conduits, guiding users to external websites or e-commerce stores. While this latter method preserves more control over branding and checkout workflows, it risks losing potential customers through additional steps or distractions. The growing preference for in-app shopping emphasizes convenience and immediacy, mirroring consumers' shifting expectations in a digitally saturated world.

A few major platforms exemplify how this social commerce model operates in practice. **Facebook Shops** launched in 2020 as a unified shopping experience across Facebook and Instagram, allowing merchants to create customized storefronts accessible directly from profiles or ads. These shops support extensive product catalogs with rich visual presentation, making it easy for users to browse and buy without leaving the app. Instagram Shopping further enhances engagement by enabling brands to tag products in posts, stories, and reels, thereby capitalizing on the platform's highly visual and influencer-driven environment. **TikTok**, too, has entered the e-commerce arena with native features that encourage impulse purchases through interactive livestreams, shoppable videos, and creator endorsements. These integrations leverage the platform's viral algorithm to introduce products organically within content feeds, blurring lines between entertainment and retail.

Behind the digital storefront lies the often overlooked

but critical component of *product catalog management*.
Sellers must upload inventory items—commonly
referred to as SKUs (stock keeping units)—each
encompassing descriptions, images, pricing, and
availability status. Effective catalog management
requires regular synchronization to reflect real-time
stock counts and avoid disappointing customers
with out-of-stock notifications. Automated tools help
streamline this process by connecting merchants' local
or cloud-based inventories directly to social platforms,
reducing errors and ensuring that promotional efforts
align with actual product offerings. Clear, appealing
product descriptions and high-quality visuals remain
indispensable; they act as the virtual handshake,
convincing users that the item will meet their needs.

Once a shopper decides to buy, the ensuing *checkout
and payment process* becomes the pivot on which the
entire experience balances. Social platforms offer *native
payment gateways* designed for speed and security,
often integrating major credit cards, digital wallets,
and alternative payment methods without requiring
customers to leave the app environment. These native
systems conform to rigorous standards like PCI DSS
(Payment Card Industry Data Security Standard)
to protect sensitive information and reduce friction
in payment entry. In some cases, platforms allow
merchants to employ *third-party payment processors*, such
as PayPal or Stripe, preserving established setups that
sellers already trust. Choosing between native and
external payment options involves trade-offs between
user convenience, control over the transaction, and
geographic availability.

Once payment is confirmed, *order fulfillment workflows*
take center stage. Platforms typically automate key
customer communications: order confirmations,

shipping updates, and delivery notifications keep buyers informed every step of the way. Integration with logistics providers allows merchants to print shipping labels, schedule pickups, and monitor shipment statuses within their dashboard, enhancing operational efficiency. Timely and transparent fulfillment dramatically influences customer satisfaction and repeat business. Some platforms further support *return management* and customer support directly through the app, closing the post-purchase loop and fostering consumer trust.

E-commerce does not exist in isolation, but rather as part of an *omnichannel strategy* that blends online, mobile, and brick-and-mortar touchpoints for a consistent customer journey. For example, a buyer might discover a product on Instagram, complete checkout via Facebook Shops on desktop, and pick up the item in a physical store. Platforms support this fluidity through features such as inventory visibility across channels, unified customer profiles, and flexible fulfillment options including curbside pickup or home delivery. This integration amplifies marketing efforts and ensures that customers can interact with a brand where and how they prefer, removing barriers between online discovery and offline experience.

Maximizing sales requires *conversion optimization*—turning casual browsers into paying customers with minimal friction. Key tactics include strategic *product tagging*, which links visual content directly to purchase options, reducing the time and effort needed to locate items. Clear *calls-to-action* embedded within posts or stories guide user behavior, inviting clicks with phrases like "Shop Now" or "Tap to Buy." Simplified checkout flows reduce abandonment by minimizing the number of screens, pre-filling information where possible, and offering multiple payment choices. Well-crafted product recommendations and social proof through reviews or influencer endorsements further enhance purchasing confidence.

Knowing which levers to pull depends on tracking *key e-commerce metrics*. The *conversion rate* measures the proportion of visitors who complete a purchase, indicating the overall effectiveness of the sales funnel. *Average order value* (AOV) reveals how much customers spend per transaction, guiding promotional strategies and bundling decisions. *Cart abandonment* rates expose where buyers hesitate or disengage, providing insight to streamline checkout or adjust messaging. Finally, *customer lifetime value* (CLV) aggregates the projected revenue a single buyer will generate over time, critical for evaluating marketing spend and loyalty initiatives. Together, these metrics form a diagnostic toolkit enabling continuous improvement.

A powerful aspect of platform-based e-commerce is the ability to leverage *customer data* for *retargeting*—serving personalized advertisements based on users' browsing and purchase behavior. By analyzing which products users viewed but did not buy, or which categories they frequent, merchants can craft targeted campaigns that appear as sponsored posts or stories designed to nudge prospects back toward conversion. This data-driven cycle optimizes advertising efficiency and nurtures customer relationships, turning one-time buyers into repeat patrons.

Bringing these elements together reveals a pathway toward social commerce success. Launching an in-platform storefront begins with selecting appropriate tools—whether Facebook Shops' comprehensive setup or TikTok's dynamic video commerce—and uploading a consistent, appealing product catalog. Enabling seamless checkout and handling fulfillment efficiently

secures positive user experiences. Maintaining an omnichannel presence broadens reach, while conversion-
focused content and calls-to-action accelerate sales.
Tracking vital metrics and harnessing customer data
for personalized retargeting create a feedback loop for
ongoing growth. With attention to these interconnected
facets, sellers can tap into the unrivaled scale and
immediacy of social platforms, transforming followers
into customers with unprecedented ease.

7.5 Customer Engagement and Support

The landscape of customer service has undergone a
profound transformation in the age of social media,
shifting from the traditional call center to dynamic,
interactive networks where brands and consumers
connect in real time. Rather than receiving help
exclusively through phone calls or emails, customers
now expect immediate, accessible support on platforms
where they spend much of their time—Facebook,
Twitter, Instagram, and emerging channels. This shift is
not merely about convenience; it reflects a fundamental
change in how companies engage with their audience,
making customer service a public, social, and influential
part of the brand experience.

Social media platforms complement, and in some
cases replace, conventional call centers by offering a
more visible and interactive form of service. Whereas
call centers handled inquiries in private and often
required lengthy waits, social channels demand swift,
transparent responses. A single tweet or comment
requesting assistance can be seen by dozens, sometimes
thousands, of followers, turning support into a public
performance. This visibility incentivizes brands to

be prompt and helpful, as missed or slow replies can
damage reputation instantaneously. Furthermore,
social networks allow companies to proactively reach
out during product launches, outages, or recalls, turning
crisis moments into demonstrations of responsiveness.

This sets a high bar for response times. Customers today
expect rapid replies—in many cases, within minutes—
especially on comments, direct messages, and chat interfaces. These expectations have driven the establishment
of service-level agreements (SLAs) specifically tailored
to social interactions. For example, many brands aim
to respond to queries within one hour during business
hours, and often faster for high-priority issues. Unlike
traditional channels where a 24-hour turnaround might
be acceptable, social media's real-time nature reshapes
the customer's tolerance for delay. Achieving these standards requires not just dedicated teams but intelligent
workflows to triage issues and ensure no request falls
through the cracks.

Automation has become indispensable in meeting these
response demands. Chatbots—programs designed to interact with customers through text—come in two main
varieties:

- Rule-based bots follow predetermined scripts to
  answer frequent, straightforward questions such
  as store hours or order status. They excel at rapid,
  consistent responses but struggle with nuance or
  complex requests.

- AI-driven bots, powered by machine learning and
  natural language processing, can handle more
  conversational exchanges, interpreting varied
  phrasing and escalating when necessary. While
  chatbots cannot yet replace human empathy, they
  serve as the first line of defense, resolving many

inquiries promptly and freeing human agents to focus on more intricate or sensitive issues.

Beyond direct brand interaction, social media fosters community forums and peer support groups that have become vital complements to formal service channels. Some brands cultivate branded user groups on platforms like Facebook or Reddit, where customers share troubleshooting tips, hacks, and experiences. These spaces transform customers into active participants in the support ecosystem, reducing service costs and creating a sense of belonging. Peer-to-peer assistance often provides faster, creative solutions that official channels may overlook, while positive interactions within these communities deepen customer loyalty and brand advocacy.

These social interactions also offer a rich source of feedback for product development. By monitoring conversations, companies gain insight into user pain points, desired features, and emerging trends. Feedback loops—where customer input is systematically collected, categorized, and routed to relevant teams—enable brands to refine their products and services continuously. For example, a surge in discussion about a specific bug on Twitter or in forums can alert developers more quickly than traditional customer surveys. Listening attentively thus transforms support channels into strategic tools for innovation rather than mere troubleshooting outlets.

Personalization is another pillar that elevates social media customer support from transactional exchanges to meaningful relationships. By integrating user profiles and historical interactions, brands tailor their responses to reflect the individual's context—such as past purchases, preferences, or previous support cases. A personalized reply not only resolves the issue more

191

efficiently but signals to customers that they are valued as individuals, not anonymous ticket numbers. This approach leverages data responsibly to deliver nuanced service, blending automation and human touch to foster genuine connection.

Inevitably, some issues escalate beyond routine inquiries, requiring clear crisis management workflows. Brands must develop protocols to identify and prioritize high-impact problems, such as widespread outages, product recalls, or legal concerns, when rapid and coordinated responses are critical. Social media's public nature demands transparency and accountability; silence or inadequate responses during crises amplify frustration and erode trust. Escalation workflows typically involve flagging critical messages for senior support staff or cross-departmental teams, drafting approved communications, and coordinating timely updates to keep customers informed. A well-managed crisis can convert potential backlash into a demonstration of reliability.

To ensure effectiveness, brands rely on robust metrics that measure customer satisfaction and support quality across social channels. Common quantitative indicators include Customer Satisfaction (CSAT) scores, which capture users' immediate feedback on a support interaction; Net Promoter Score (NPS), gauging overall loyalty and likelihood to recommend; and resolution rates, reflecting how many inquiries are fully addressed within a given timeframe. Complementing these are qualitative inputs—open-ended feedback, sentiment analysis, and social listening—that provide nuance and context. Together, these metrics enable continuous improvement and reinforce accountability.

Integrating social interactions with customer relationship management (CRM) systems completes the modern support ecosystem. Social CRM involves syncing conversations from platforms into centralized databases and helpdesk software, creating unified customer profiles accessible across departments. This integration ensures that agents can see a customer's full history, preferences, and prior engagements, regardless of channel, and respond in a coherent, informed manner. It also facilitates automation triggers and analytics, linking social insights with sales, marketing, and development efforts to create a seamless customer experience.

This convergence of methods—rapid social responsiveness, intelligent automation, community empowerment, feedback integration, personalized engagement, crisis protocols, outcome-focused metrics, and CRM synchronization—charts a comprehensive approach to customer support in the social age. Together, these practices transform service from a mere cost center into a strategic driver of loyalty, brand equity, and continuous innovation. Companies that master this interplay ensure that every interaction not only resolves problems but builds lasting relationships, turning customers from bystanders into advocates in the digital marketplace.

7.6 Entrepreneurship and New Opportunities

The rise of social platforms has not only transformed how we communicate but has also fundamentally reshaped entrepreneurship. No longer confined to traditional storefronts or corporate hierarchies, new business models and entrepreneurial paths now spring directly from the digital ecosystems where billions connect. These platforms have unlocked unprecedented opportunities for individuals and small teams to create, market, and monetize ideas with speed, agility, and global reach. Understanding this landscape requires diving into the emerging structures that the creator economy, crowdfunding, gig work, and other digital innovations enable.

At the heart of this transformation lies the *creator economy*, a term encapsulating individuals who leverage social platforms to build audiences and monetize their content directly. Unlike conventional media professionals, creators use tools—video, podcasts, blogs, photo-sharing apps—to craft unique value around their personalities, expertise, or entertainment. Income streams flow from advertising revenue shares, sponsored content, merchandise sales, and premium memberships. This shift democratizes economic power, allowing anyone with talent and tenacity to participate in content creation without gatekeepers like studios or publishers. For example, platforms such as YouTube, TikTok, and Instagram foster creators who can scale from niche passions to substantial businesses, sometimes earning millions annually. The creator economy represents an entrepreneurial revolution where audiences are both product and customer, and brand building is a continuous, intimate dialogue.

Complementing this is the rise of *crowdfunding and patronage models*, which have become vital for financing creative work, inventions, and social causes without traditional investment channels. Platforms like Kickstarter introduced a new paradigm: creators pitch projects directly to prospective backers worldwide, who support them with upfront funds in exchange for rewards or early access. This removes dependency on banks or investors, enabling grassroots innovation. Patreon, by contrast, implements subscription-based patronage, where fans contribute small amounts regularly to support ongoing creation—imagine a digital tip jar aligned with content calendars. These models empower entrepreneurs to validate ideas, mobilize communities, and sustain projects early on, reducing financial risk and fostering transparency between producers and supporters.

Another powerful force reshaping entrepreneurship is the growth of the *gig economy and micro-services*, which harness freelance platforms to connect task-specific talent to markets instantly. Websites like Upwork, Fiverr, and TaskRabbit break down work into discrete projects—designing a logo, editing a video, managing social media accounts—that freelancers worldwide compete to fulfill. This micro-tasking approach is flexible and accessible, making entrepreneurship a highly individualized pursuit without massive overheads or long-term commitments. It also blurs the lines between consumer and entrepreneur; anyone with a skill can monetize it on demand, supported by rating systems and streamlined payments. This shift expands possibilities for micro-entrepreneurs who rely on their skills and online reputation rather than traditional firm structures.

Layered onto these individual efforts are *platform-based startup models* that emerge primarily through social channels. Direct-to-consumer (DTC) brands built on Instagram or TikTok bypass wholesalers and brick-and-mortar stores, reaching customers with highly targeted, authentic messaging. This model reduces barriers to entry, lowers costs, and accelerates feedback loops. Brands like Glossier and Gymshark grew from social media savvy communities into internationally recognized companies without traditional retail dynamics. By weaving storytelling,

195

user-generated content, and influencer partnerships
into their marketing strategies, these startups scale
efficiently while maintaining close ties to their audience.
This approach upends traditional supply chains and
marketing campaigns, proving that nimble, networked
entrepreneurship thrives in digital marketplaces.

Crucially, many of these ventures embrace *community-
driven product development*, a participatory approach
where customers help shape the products they want.
Social platforms facilitate continuous dialogue—
through comments, polls, direct messages, and forums—
enabling entrepreneurs to test concepts, gauge demand,
and iterate rapidly before large-scale launches. This
not only minimizes wasted effort but deepens loyalty
as consumers feel invested in the process. Pre-sale
campaigns financed via crowdfunding are often the first
stage of this interaction, validating product-market fit
while raising capital. The iterative process mirrors agile
software development but extends naturally to physical
goods, services, and content. By involving communities
early and transparently, entrepreneurs build resilience
and relevance.

Behind these ventures lies a growing sophistication
in *analytics and growth hacking*. Entrepreneurs today
experiment leanly—testing campaigns, product
features, or messaging using small data sets to
optimize performance quickly. Techniques such as
cohort analysis track how different user groups behave
over time, revealing retention patterns and revenue
potentials to guide decisions. Social platforms' built-in
analytics tools, coupled with third-party software,
enable tracking of engagement, conversion, and viral
spread, informing targeted growth strategies. The
concept of viral loops—where satisfied users bring in
more users in an exponential cascade—complements

paid acquisitions and organic growth. These data-driven tactics allow startups to scale efficiently, often dismantling old notions that entrepreneurship is purely guesswork or intuition.

As enterprises mature, *business model diversification* becomes a critical strategic choice. Some entrepreneurs expand horizontally, adding new product lines or services to broaden market reach and reduce dependence on a single revenue stream. Others deepen their core offerings by developing premium tiers, complementary digital goods, or enhanced customer experiences. Both paths carry trade-offs between complexity, brand coherence, and operational focus. The flexibility social platforms offer allows many to test multiple models rapidly, pivot if needed, and mix monetization techniques—from advertising to subscriptions, merchandise, or licensing—creating resilient income portfolios. This diversification often distinguishes ventures that thrive sustainably from those vulnerable to platform policy changes or evolving consumer tastes.

However, navigating this terrain requires attention to *legal considerations* that digital entrepreneurs may overlook initially. Intellectual property rights—copyrights, trademarks, patents—protect creative works, brand identities, and inventions, but require deliberate action. Content shared on social platforms is vulnerable to misuse or replication without proper safeguards. Compliance with privacy laws, advertising guidelines, and labor regulations is also essential, especially as micro-entrepreneurs shift toward employee-like roles or cross-border transactions. Contractual clarity with collaborators, clients, or sponsors prevents common disputes. While social platforms empower entrepreneurs with access and scale, legal literacy remains a foundational pillar to safeguard their innovations and reputations.

Numerous success stories highlight the potential of these new entrepreneurial paths when executed thoughtfully. Consider the journey of *Emma Chamberlain*, whose irreverent, candid vlogging style attracted millions, translating into sponsorship deals, a coffee brand, and fashion collaborations. Or *Peloton*, which began as a community-driven fitness startup leveraging social sharing to build a passionate base before disrupting traditional gym models. Smaller ventures prove equally instructive; a craftsperson might use Patreon to fund monthly project series, or a freelance illustrator expand offerings through Fiverr's marketplace, evolving customer relationships into brand-building opportunities. The common thread lies in their embrace of audience engagement, platform tools, and iterative growth informed by data and feedback.

Taken together, these entrepreneurial pathways illustrate a digital age where barriers to entry are lower but competition and complexity remain formidable. Aspiring entrepreneurs must blend creativity, strategic thinking, and community-building—leveraging social platforms not only as marketing channels but as ecosystems for product development and revenue generation. The interplay of direct audience relationships, new funding models, flexible labor arrangements, and rapid experimentation creates an environment rich in opportunity but demanding in adaptability. Success hinges on recognizing that entrepreneurship today is less about fixed blueprints and more about dynamic engagement, relentless learning, and evolving business architecture.

The landscape of entrepreneurship enabled by social platforms is vibrant and diverse, offering routes that range from solo creators monetizing personal brands to startups building global communities around novel products. These new models democratize economic opportunity while redefining the nature of work, creativity, and commerce. Understanding the mechanisms underpinning the creator economy, crowdfunding dynamics, gig work, and platform-based growth illuminates how individuals and enterprises seize new opportunities amid continuous digital transformation.

Chapter 8

Challenges, Ethics, and the Future of Social Media

In this concluding chapter, we confront the pressing challenges and ethical dilemmas posed by social media, and envision pathways toward a more equitable, sustainable, and user-centric digital future. We begin with privacy and data-protection frameworks, then assess regulatory and platform responsibilities. Next, we analyze disparities in access and representation, followed by the environmental footprint of digital infrastructure. We then survey emerging technologies, propose design and governance models for healthier platforms, and empower readers to act as ethical stewards of the digital society.

8.1 Privacy and Data Protection

Digital privacy stands at the crossroads of personal autonomy and the vast architectures of the information age. At its core, it concerns the control individuals have over their personal data—the digital footprints they unwittingly or deliberately leave scattered across platforms, devices, and networks. Personal data might include anything from names and email addresses to browsing habits, location histories, health records, and even biometric identifiers. Privacy, in this context, is not merely about secrecy but about informational autonomy: the right to decide when, how, and to what extent one's information is shared and used. This autonomy hinges upon consent—a mechanism intended to give individuals agency over their data. Yet, as we delve deeper, we discover that consent is neither straightforward nor universal; it is embedded in complex legal, social, and technological frameworks that shape the contours of privacy in the digital realm.

The journey of our data begins with its collection, a process pervasive yet often invisible. Common methods include the humble cookie on a website— small fragments of code that remember previous visits and preferences—as well as tracking pixels that silently report back user interactions, APIs linking disparate services, and myriad device permissions demanding access to cameras, microphones, contacts, and more. Each of these tools enables companies and third parties to assemble detailed profiles of individuals, refining advertising, tailoring content, or, at times, surveillance. While users might glimpse cookie banners appearing with a click, the deeper mechanisms—like device fingerprinting or cross-site tracking—remain largely opaque. Thus, data collection is seldom a simple transaction; it is a layered process that challenges the practical limits of user awareness and control.

Understanding whether such data flows respect privacy requires adopting the lens of *contextual integrity*. This concept, developed by philosopher Helen Nissenbaum, reminds us that privacy is not about total secrecy but about respecting socially established norms that govern appropriate information sharing within distinct contexts. For instance, sharing your medical history with a healthcare provider fits the norms of the medical context but sharing that same information with a social media platform breaches these expectations. Similarly, your shopping preferences shared with an online retailer may be appropriate; broad dissemination to unrelated third parties violates the principle of appropriate flow. Contextual integrity thus offers a nuanced framework, highlighting that privacy violations stem not simply from data collection, but from breaches in the norms that dictate where, how, and for what purposes data should travel.

Central to maintaining this integrity is the model of consent. Consent mechanisms come in various flavors, two of the most recognizable being opt-in and opt-out. An opt-in model requires explicit permission before personal data collection or use, placing power firmly with the user but often at the cost of friction and user experience. In contrast, opt-out assumes consent by default and requires the user to actively withdraw it, a practice that has drawn criticism for exploiting user inattention or confusion. Achieving nuanced user control also involves granular permission settings where users can specify different levels of access—for example, allowing a navigation app to access location data only while in use, but not continuously. These models reflect ongoing tensions between usability, business interests, and privacy rights, and their design profoundly shapes how much true control users possess.

Yet consent does not operate in a vacuum; it must be supported by *transparency*—clear, accessible communication about data practices. Privacy policies have traditionally been dense, legalistic texts that few actually read, let alone understand. Efforts to improve transparency advocate for concise summaries, layered notices that present important points upfront, and machine-readable formats that enable software tools to parse and compare privacy terms automatically. Transparency serves two vital purposes: informing users to make reasoned decisions about their data, and fostering trust by demonstrating accountability. Without it, consent becomes hollow, mere compliance rather than meaningful empowerment.

Even when best practices are followed, the risk of data breaches—unauthorized access, theft, or loss of personal data—persists. Vulnerabilities arise from software bugs, misconfigured servers, insider threats, or sophisticated hacking. When breaches occur, companies face obligations to notify affected users promptly and transparently, allowing individuals to take protective measures such as changing passwords or monitoring financial accounts. Remediation may involve offering credit monitoring services, legal recourse, or improving security architectures to prevent recurrence. The prevalence of such incidents underscores the necessity of robust data protection strategies that extend beyond mere promises to technical and organizational safeguards.

One such safeguard is *anonymization*, a set of techniques designed to sever personal data from direct identifiers to protect individual identity while enabling valuable data use. Basic methods include *pseudonymization*, which replaces identifiers with reversible codes, and *aggregation*, combining data into summaries that obscure individual details. However, anonymization has limits; advances in data analytics and the availability of external datasets can sometimes re-identify supposedly anonymous records. This tension between utility and privacy demands constant vigilance and evolving standards to mitigate re-identification risks.

The global landscape of data protection has transformed

remarkably in recent years, driven by landmark legal frameworks such as the European Union's General Data Protection Regulation (GDPR) and California's Consumer Privacy Act (CCPA). These regulations define stringent requirements for data collection, processing, and user rights—including the right to access, correct, and delete personal data. GDPR, for example, imposes hefty fines for non-compliance and mandates principles like data minimization and purpose limitation. Meanwhile, other regions are crafting tailored laws that reflect local values and concerns, reflecting a patchwork of protections that increasingly shape corporate data practices worldwide. These legal frameworks represent a critical shift towards recognizing personal data as an extension of individual sovereignty.

To embed privacy at the heart of technology, the principle of *privacy by design* advocates integrating privacy considerations into every stage of product development rather than retrofitting protections after deployment. This approach encourages practices such as defaulting to privacy-friendly settings, minimizing data collection, employing encryption, and conducting privacy impact assessments early and often. Privacy by design aligns technical innovation with ethical responsibility, ensuring that new functionalities do not come at the cost of eroding user rights or trust.

Ultimately, safeguarding privacy and data protection relies on a combination of technological safeguards, legal oversight, informed user participation, and ethical corporate behaviour. Best practices emphasize user-centric data management: empowering individuals with meaningful control, maintaining transparency, and ensuring accountability through clear policies and responsive support. Trust is the currency in this domain, earned by re-

205

specting contextual norms, preparing for and managing risks, and embedding privacy deeply into digital ecosystems. As data permeates ever more facets of life, our collective commitment to these principles will determine whether digital spaces become environments of empowerment or exploitation.

8.2 Regulation and Platform Responsibility

As digital platforms grow ever larger and more influential, the question of how to govern their activities—especially content moderation and algorithmic decision-making—has become a pressing concern. Unlike traditional publishers or broadcasters, platforms operate within a complex web of legal, ethical, and commercial obligations, often navigating murky waters where free speech, public safety, and corporate interests collide. This section unpacks the major models of platform accountability, the inherent challenges in content moderation, and the evolving landscape of legal and ethical oversight.

At the core of platform governance lie three broad frameworks: *self-regulation*, *co-regulation*, and *statutory oversight*. Self-regulation entrusts platforms with the responsibility to set and enforce their own rules and standards, often motivated by reputational concerns and market pressures. Such policies may be formalized as community guidelines or codes of conduct. Co-regulation introduces a collaborative element, pairing government or external stakeholders with platforms to jointly develop policies and implementation strategies. This approach seeks to balance flexibility with accountability. Lastly, statutory oversight involves direct legislative mandates, which compel platforms to adhere to specific obligations, backed by enforcement mechanisms such as fines or injunctions. Each model carries distinct trade-offs between agility, legitimacy, and enforceability.

One of the thorniest issues these frameworks face is the sheer scale and complexity of content moderation. Platforms host billions of users, generating vast quantities of user-generated content every second. Human review, though nuanced and context-aware, is practically impossible to apply consistently at this scale. Automated systems and artificial intelligence offer speed and consistency but often struggle to capture subtleties of context, cultural norms, irony, or sarcasm. For example, an automated filter might mistakenly remove a valid criticism of government policy because it contains provocative language, whereas a human moderator could better assess intent and nuance. Moreover, moderation decisions must grapple with disparate cultural, legal, and linguistic environments, making a one-size-fits-all approach impractical. This tension between human judgment and technological efficiency underscores much of the ongoing debate in platform responsibility.

Balancing freedom of expression and harm reduction lies at the philosophical heart of regulation. Platforms serve as modern public squares, championing free speech and democratic engagement. Yet, they are also arenas where misinformation, hate speech, harassment, and coordinated abuse flourish, sometimes with real-world consequences. Striking this balance is precarious: overly aggressive censorship risks stifling dissent and marginalizing voices; lax moderation may allow harm to proliferate unchecked. Platforms therefore walk a tightrope, calibrating their policies to protect vulnerable groups and public interests without morphing into

207

state-like censors or opaque gatekeepers. This dynamic evokes broader societal questions about the limits of speech, the role of private actors in safeguarding democracy, and how global norms can harmonize diverse values.

Several key legal instruments underpin the evolving regulatory environment. In the United States, Section 230 of the Communications Decency Act has been foundational, granting platforms immunity from liability for user-generated content while permitting good-faith content removal. This provision has been both praised for enabling innovation and critiqued for allowing platforms to evade responsibility. Meanwhile, the European Union has pioneered comprehensive regulation through the Digital Services Act (DSA), which imposes transparency requirements, risk assessments, and stricter obligations on very large platforms. Other jurisdictions have begun introducing laws targeting hate speech, misinformation, or algorithmic fairness, reflecting a patchwork yet intensifying global effort to hold platforms accountable.

To foster accountability and public trust, transparency reporting is increasingly mandated or volunteered by platforms. Transparency reports typically disclose statistics on content takedowns, government requests for data or censorship, and advertising archives. Some platforms now publish algorithmic audits or summaries explaining how recommendation systems function and how they are audited for bias or harm. This expanded openness offers external stakeholders—users, regulators, and civil society—a window into platform operations that were previously opaque. However, the depth and accessibility of these reports vary widely, and critics argue that without independent verification, transparency risks becoming a performative gesture rather than a tool for meaningful oversight.

Algorithmic accountability has emerged as a critical frontier. As automated systems increasingly shape what content surfaces to users, questions about fairness, bias, and explainability have moved to the forefront. Calls for *explainable AI* seek to unpack the "black box" nature of algorithms, enabling users and regulators to understand why certain content is promoted or demoted. Bias audits aim to detect and mitigate discriminatory patterns embedded unintentionally in training data or design choices. Some proposals advocate for publicly overseen algorithmic impact assessments, akin to environmental reviews, to anticipate and address potential harms before deployment. These efforts represent a shift toward treating algorithms as governance actors themselves, requiring scrutiny alongside human decisions.

Corporate ethics boards, codes of conduct, and stakeholder engagement are increasingly influential components of platform governance, highlighting the role of *ethical design* and internal self-reflection. Some companies have established dedicated ethics committees to guide product development and shape content policies, seeking to embed moral considerations directly into business strategies. Codes of conduct often articulate commitments to diversity, equity, and user safety, while stakeholder consultations bring in perspectives from civil society, academia, and affected communities. Although these mechanisms vary in effectiveness and independence, they signal a growing recognition that corporate responsibility extends beyond legal compliance, aspiring toward a form of digital citizenship.

Multistakeholder policymaking captures the emerging consensus that no single actor can effectively regulate platform activity alone. Governments wield regulatory power, but lack the technical expertise or agile responsiveness platforms possess. Civil society advocates bring human rights and public interest perspectives but depend on access and influence. Platforms offer essential operational knowledge and market leverage but face conflicts of interest. Collaborative governance models attempt to leverage these complementary strengths through dialogue, joint initiatives, and co-created standards. Examples include forums like the Global Internet Forum to Counter Terrorism or voluntary coalitions addressing harassment and misinformation. Such pluralistic approaches aim to build both legitimacy and efficacy, though success depends on sustained commitment, transparency, and mutual trust.

Enforcement and compliance mechanisms give teeth to regulatory frameworks. Legislators may impose fines calibrated to a platform's revenue, issue injunctions compelling specific actions, or authorize investigations and audits. Voluntary certification programs offer another path, encouraging platforms to meet industry-developed standards in exchange for public trust marks or reduced regulatory scrutiny. The challenge lies in achieving enforcement that is predictable, proportionate, and adaptive to fast-moving technological realities. Overly punitive measures risk chilling innovation or fragmenting markets, while weak enforcement invites regulatory capture or noncompliance. Striking the right equilibrium remains an ongoing quest within legal and policy circles.

Taken together, these diverse regulatory strategies reveal both potential and limitation. Self-regulation provides agility and operational insight but can lack transparency and accountability. Statutory oversight promises legitimacy and enforcement power but may struggle with adaptability and unintended consequences. Co-regulation and multistakeholder governance offer promising hybrids but require effective partnership management. Transparency, algorithmic audits, and ethical design pave new ground in understanding and shaping platform impacts, yet their real-world effects hinge on rigorous implementation and inclusive participation. The journey toward balancing innovation, freedom, safety, and fairness in digital spaces is far from complete, demanding continuous dialogue and creative experimentation across all sectors of society.

8.3 Inequality and Access Issues

The promise of digital technologies to connect the world and democratize information often encounters a stubborn obstacle: inequality. Far from a level playing field, access to the internet and digital platforms is riddled with disparities, shaping who participates, who benefits, and who remains on the outside looking in. These gaps manifest across global regions, socioeconomic strata, demographic groups, and even within the design of the platforms themselves. Understanding and addressing these inequalities is essential to creating a truly inclusive digital society.

At the broadest scale, the global digital divide remains a fundamental hurdle. While urban centers in wealthier nations enjoy high-speed broadband and ubiquitous smartphone use, many regions—especially in parts of Africa, South Asia, and Latin America—struggle with limited infrastructure, patchy network coverage, and a scarcity of devices. This divide goes beyond mere connectivity; it includes the quality of access, with many users relying on slow, expensive, or unreliable connec-

tions that restrict the full promise of digital participation.
Device ownership itself can be a barrier; millions rely
on outdated phones or share single devices among large
families. This infrastructural disparity erects an invisible but formidable wall between those with immediate,
seamless digital engagement and those relegated to intermittent or minimal access.

Socioeconomic and demographic factors compound
these divides. Income shapes not only the ability to
afford devices and services but also affects digital
literacy, educational opportunities, and the time
available to engage online. Lower-income individuals
often prioritize necessities over technology investments,
while education plays a critical role in shaping digital
skills and confidence. Older adults frequently encounter
difficulties adapting to evolving technologies, either
due to lack of exposure or physical constraints, which
limits their participation. These intersections of income,
education, and age create layered barriers—those who
might benefit most from digital inclusion often face the
greatest obstacles to engagement.

Geography also plays a decisive role, as urban–rural
divides starkly illustrate. Cities typically enjoy dense
network infrastructure, a competitive market of service
providers, and widespread Wi-Fi hotspots. In contrast,
rural areas—sometimes just a few dozen miles away—
must contend with fewer cell towers, longer distances
between communications nodes, and often prohibitive
costs of infrastructure maintenance. The result is a
paradox where rural populations may rely on slower
or less reliable connections, affecting everything
from education and healthcare access to economic
opportunities and civic participation. The rural digital
divide is not just about technology; it is a reflection
of broader patterns of investment and development,

leaving whole communities less empowered in the digital era.

Within these communities are further fractures shaped by gender and minority status. Globally, women are less likely to own digital devices or have internet access compared to men, a gap rooted in cultural norms, economic constraints, and safety concerns. Minority groups—whether defined by ethnicity, language, or religion—often face additional barriers, including limited content in their languages and discriminatory practices that curtail their voice. Economic marginalization intertwines with cultural factors, restricting who can participate fully and whose perspectives shape digital spaces. In many cases, this exclusion is self-reinforcing, as underrepresented groups see fewer role models and resources reflecting their experiences, making digital engagement less inviting.

Disability is another frontier where access divides remain pronounced. While many platforms now incorporate assistive technologies—such as captions on videos, alt text for images, and voice interfaces—implementation is inconsistent, and gaps persist. Users with visual, auditory, cognitive, or motor disabilities may encounter content that is inaccessible, poorly designed, or unadapted to their needs. The digital environment should be an equalizer, but neglecting accessibility features perpetuates exclusion, limiting opportunities for education, employment, socialization, and advocacy among disabled individuals.

Language and cultural inclusion add yet another layer of complexity. The dominance of a handful of major languages, notably English, on the internet sidelines speakers of less widely used tongues. Creating quality, engaging content in multiple languages requires resources and cultural sensitivity that many organizations struggle to provide. Moreover, cultural nuances affect how information is framed and interpreted, making straightforward translations insufficient for meaningful inclusion. Without genuine localization efforts, large segments of the world's population remain underrepresented or misrepresented online, narrowing the diversity of voices and knowledge shared digitally.

Even as connectivity and content improve, the design of algorithms and platforms can inadvertently widen divides. Data-driven models often reflect and amplify existing biases, skewing visibility and recommendations in ways that marginalize certain communities. For example, automated content filtering may disproportionately flag posts from minority groups or activists, while language processing tools might underperform with dialects different from the training data. This algorithmic bias constrains participation, subtly excluding or misrepresenting voices, and complicating efforts to foster equitable engagement.

Underlying all these issues are disparities in digital literacy—the skills needed to navigate, evaluate, create, and critique online content effectively. Digital literacy is not merely about technical proficiency but involves critical thinking, privacy awareness, and the ability to participate meaningfully. Skill gaps often mirror socioeconomic and educational inequalities, with disadvantaged groups less equipped to harness the benefits of digital platforms or to protect themselves from misinformation and exploitation. Promoting equitable digital literacy is thus crucial for bridging participation gaps and empowering users across society.

Several strategies have emerged to bridge these divides and foster more inclusive access. Community networks are one promising approach: locally owned and operated infrastructure tailored to the specific needs of a region, especially where commercial providers have little incentive to invest. Public–private partnerships harness resources and expertise from governments, NGOs, and corporations to subsidize connectivity and digital skills programs. Innovations in low-cost devices and offline-capable applications address affordability and infrastructure challenges. Education initiatives focusing on digital literacy and inclusion aim to equip marginalized groups with tools to engage confidently and safely online. Importantly, these efforts recognize that technical solutions alone are insufficient; addressing structural inequalities, cultural sensitivities, and ongoing support is key to sustainable progress.

Ultimately, fostering equity in digital participation requires a holistic and coordinated approach. This means ensuring affordable, reliable infrastructure while investing in inclusive design and content creation; promoting policies that encourage participation from underrepresented groups; combating algorithmic biases; and advancing education that builds critical skills. The digital landscape is not defined solely by technology but shaped by social, economic, and political forces. Bridging divides is not just about connecting devices, but connecting people—amplifying diverse voices, expanding opportunities, and building a digital world that reflects the richness of global humanity.

8.4 Sustainability and Environmental Impact

Behind the seamless connection and viral moments on social media lies a vast, often invisible digital infrastructure with a substantial ecological footprint. From sprawling data centers humming with servers

to the smartphones perched in our hands, the
environmental impact of the social media ecosystem is
complex and multifaceted. Understanding this footprint
requires looking beyond the screen to the energy use,
manufacturing processes, and user behaviors that
together shape social media's sustainability profile.

Data centers are the beating hearts of social media platforms, housing the servers that store, process, and deliver immense volumes of information. These facilities
consume vast quantities of electricity—not only to power
the servers themselves but also to cool the heat they generate. Estimates suggest that the global data center industry accounts for roughly 1% of the world's electricity consumption, with a considerable share dedicated to
social media and other cloud-based services. Cooling
systems alone can consume up to 40% of a data center's
power usage, making efficient thermal management a
critical factor in reducing environmental impact. Network equipment, routers, and switches further draw energy as data traverses the internet, adding layers to this
invisible energy cascade.

Yet, the footprint extends upstream to the production
and eventual disposal of the physical devices we use to
access social media. Smartphones, tablets, and laptops
carry an environmental cost embedded in their lifecycles.
Manufacturing these devices involves the extraction of
rare earth minerals and substantial energy inputs, contributing to carbon emissions, water usage, and habitat
disruption. The relentless push for the latest model fuels
planned obsolescence, encouraging frequent device replacement and amplifying manufacturing impacts. Recycling, though a promising solution, faces significant
challenges: the complexity of extracting valuable materials, lack of standardized e-waste processing, and limited
consumer participation all hinder effective resource re-

covery. As a result, only a minority of discarded devices are properly refurbished or recycled, leading to mountains of electronic waste accumulating worldwide.

Electronic waste (e-waste) poses a particular environmental challenge. The sheer volume generated annually—estimated at over 50 million metric tons globally—includes countless social media access devices. Informal recycling sectors in developing countries often resort to hazardous techniques such as open-air burning or acid baths, releasing toxic substances and polluting air, water, and soil. Even in developed nations, bottlenecks in collection infrastructure and economic viability limit the scale of responsible refurbishment or resale programs. Consequently, the linear consumer cycle of "buy, use, discard" exacerbates resource depletion and environmental degradation.

User behavior amplifies the environmental footprint in less obvious yet significant ways. Streaming videos, sharing images, uploading stories, and the constant syncing of apps in the background all demand data transmission and processing. Video streaming alone accounts for roughly 60% of internet traffic, and as video content dominates social media feeds, its energy cost rises correspondingly. Even seemingly innocuous actions like auto-play videos, endless scrolling, and data-heavy emojis accumulate into substantial energy use and carbon emissions. The responsiveness expected from social media platforms encourages continuous server engagement, compounding energy demands.

Addressing these challenges has sparked a range of green computing practices within the tech industry. Energy-efficient hardware development targets components with lower power draw without sacrificing performance. Virtualization—running multiple virtual servers on a single physical machine—improves utilization rates, reducing the need for excess physical servers. Load-balancing strategies ensure data center workloads are distributed to maximize energy efficiency, often shifting non-urgent tasks to off-peak times. These advanced techniques, alongside thermal design innovations, help curb data centers' environmental toll, though their adoption varies across providers.

Renewable energy integration emerges as a transformative solution underpinning greener data centers. Tech giants increasingly power facilities with solar, wind, or hydroelectric sources, aiming to achieve carbon neutrality or even net positive impacts. For instance, some leading social media platforms operate data centers entirely on renewable energy, taking advantage of location-specific resources and long-term green power purchase agreements. This shift not only reduces operational carbon emissions but also sends market signals encouraging broader renewable energy adoption.

Complementing energy concerns, circular economy models seek to close the loop on device lifecycles. Initiatives such as device buyback programs, refurbishment efforts, and parts reuse aim to extend product life and reduce e-waste generation. Companies offer trade-in incentives, refurbish returned hardware for resale, and recycle precious materials economically. These programs embody a systemic rethinking—prioritizing resource conservation and waste minimization over disposable consumerism. However, scaling these models requires cross-sector collaboration, consumer awareness, and regulatory support to overcome logistical and economic barriers.

Sustainable software design complements hardware and energy strategies by minimizing the digital load that social media places on infrastructure. Thoughtful data

218

retention policies limit the accumulation of unnecessary data, reducing storage and backup demands. Code optimization ensures applications run efficiently, requiring less computational power. Emerging delay-tolerant architectures allow non-time-critical data processing to occur during periods of lower energy demand or cleaner energy availability. Together, these software approaches reduce server workloads and network traffic, shrinking the environmental footprint of everyday user interactions.

Transparency and accountability in environmental stewardship receive growing attention through ESG (Environmental, Social, and Governance) reporting. Social media platforms and parent companies increasingly disclose their energy consumption, emissions, and sustainability initiatives according to established frameworks. These reports provide stakeholders, including users and investors, with insights into what companies are doing to reduce impact. ESG reporting fosters competitive pressures, incentivizing platforms to innovate in sustainability and address supply chain concerns more thoroughly.

As the digital and physical worlds intertwine ever more tightly, social media's ecological footprint becomes impossible to ignore. Best practices for reducing environmental harm span technical innovation, responsible corporate policies, and conscientious user behaviors. The combined efforts of renewable-powered data centers, efficient device lifecycles, optimized software, and transparent impact reporting chart a course toward a more sustainable social media ecosystem. Yet, the challenge remains formidable, requiring systemic change and collective responsibility to ensure that the joy of connection does not come at the planet's expense.

8.5 Emerging Technologies and Trends

The landscape of social experiences is undergoing a radical transformation fueled by a suite of next-generation technologies. These innovations do not simply add new features; they fundamentally reshape how we connect, share, and build communities in digital spaces. From the quiet revolution of artificial intelligence that personalizes our interactions to the expansive promise of persistent virtual worlds, emerging technologies are redefining the texture of social life.

At the forefront of this change are advances in artificial intelligence (AI), where generative models have unlocked new possibilities for creativity and communication. Models like GPT and diffusion-based image generators can craft text, audio, and visuals with astonishing fluency, enriching social content with personalized flair. Personalization engines now tailor feeds and recommendations with refined sensitivity to individual preferences, creating experiences that feel uniquely attuned to each user. On the moderation front, AI-powered systems sift through vast digital conversations in real time, flagging harmful or inappropriate content to foster safer online spaces—though this raises ongoing debates about bias, transparency, and the limits of automated judgment.

Parallel to AI's invisible scaffolding are the vividly visible realms of augmented reality (AR) and virtual reality (VR). These immersive environments elevate social interaction from flat screens to spatial experiences: friends gather around a virtual campfire, colleagues collaborate on a 3D blueprint, and fans attend concerts without leaving their homes. AR layers digital elements seamlessly over the physical world, enriching our surroundings with context-aware information, while VR creates entirely fabricated environments that transport users elsewhere. Advances in hardware—lightweight headsets, improved motion tracking, and better haptic feedback—are steadily lowering the barriers to entry, making these technologies practical not just for gamers or early adopters but for everyday social engagement.

A complementary technical shift empowers users behind the scenes: federated and decentralized networks. Unlike traditional platforms that centralize data and control, these architectures enable communication and content sharing across many independent servers. Protocols such as ActivityPub exemplify this federated approach, allowing users on different software to interact as if part of one vast social ecosystem. Blockchain-based identity systems further enhance this paradigm by giving people sovereign control over their digital identities and assets, securing privacy while fostering trust without relying on gatekeepers. The promise here is a user-centric internet where data ownership, rather than corporate oversight, drives social exchange.

Interwoven with these architectural shifts is the evolving concept of the *metaverse*. Far from a single platform, the metaverse envisions an interconnected network of persistent virtual worlds—places that exist continuously, evolve through user participation, and accommodate a variety of activities. Here, avatars become more than static profile pictures; they serve as expressive, customizable digital beings that carry reputations and identities across environments. Crucial to this vision is asset interoperability, the ability for digital goods like clothing, artwork, or currency to move seamlessly between different metaverse spaces. This fluidity holds the potential to revolutionize digital economies and social capital, blurring boundaries between gaming, commerce, and community.

Realizing many of these technologies requires robust infrastructure, particularly in networking and computation. Edge computing, combined with the widespread deployment of 5G networks, is a key enabler. By moving data processing closer to users and harnessing ultra-fast, low-latency connections, edge computing allows social applications to respond instantly and adapt to context—think live location-aware augmented reality chats or real-time multiplayer experiences free from frustrating lag. This physical decentralization of compute power supports ambitious, highly interactive social environments that were previously impractical due to network constraints.

Yet, alongside the opportunities offered by synthetic media—images, videos, and audio generated or manipulated by AI—come significant risks. Deepfakes and AI-generated voices can convincingly impersonate individuals, sowing confusion, disinformation, and distrust. Detection technologies and verification protocols have become essential countermeasures in this arms race, aiming to preserve authenticity and safeguard public discourse. These developments highlight the broader challenge of aligning technological innovation with ethical imperatives: the more powerful our tools become, the greater the need to manage their unintended consequences.

Privacy, long a concern in digital social spaces, is now receiving renewed attention through advanced privacy-enhancing technologies. Differential privacy injects carefully calibrated noise into datasets to protect individual identities while allowing meaningful analysis. Secure multiparty computation enables multiple parties to jointly process data without exposing their inputs, and zero-knowledge proofs allow a user to demonstrate a fact without revealing the underlying information. These innovations enable richer social interactions and data sharing without sacrificing control over personal information, shifting the balance toward user empowerment.

Ethical AI frameworks are emerging to guide the deployment of intelligent systems in social contexts. Key principles—fairness, accountability, transparency—aim to mitigate biases and ensure that AI benefits all users equitably. Human-in-the-loop designs retain human oversight where automated decisions have significant social impact, recognizing that some judgments require empathy and contextual understanding that machines lack. By integrating ethics into the technological fabric, these frameworks set the stage for more trustworthy, inclusive social platforms.

The accelerating pace of innovation owes much to community-driven efforts. Open-source projects and decentralized governance experiments empower users and developers to collaboratively shape technology and policy. These grassroots movements challenge traditional top-down control, inviting diverse voices to contribute to the evolution of social platforms. The resulting ecosystems often reflect broader social values— privacy, freedom of expression, shared ownership—and demonstrate alternative models of innovation that emphasize transparency and collective responsibility.

Looking ahead, the convergence of these emerging technologies paints a picture of social media that is simultaneously more immersive, personalized, and user-empowered. AI will continue to enhance creativity and moderation, AR and VR will blur lines between physical and digital worlds, and decentralized architectures will return ownership of data and identity to individuals. However, this transformation is not

without peril: synthetic media threatens trust, privacy
risks endure, and ethical challenges multiply as systems
grow more complex and autonomous.

Together, these trends invite us to rethink what social
interaction means in a digital age—not as passive
consumption of content, but as active participation in
vibrant, persistent, and interconnected communities.
Navigating this terrain will require vigilance, innovation,
and a commitment to aligning technology's power with
human values. In doing so, the next generation of social
platforms may not only reshape how we connect but
also redefine the very nature of society itself.

8.6   Building a Healthier Social Media Ecosystem

The quest for healthier social media platforms begins
with a clear understanding of what constitutes
ecosystem health.   Unlike biological environments,
the vitality of social media depends on the well-being
of its users, the trust they place in the platforms, and
the inclusiveness of engagement practices.   Metrics
such as user psychological health, perceived fairness,
and equitable participation help define this landscape.
These are not merely abstract ideals; they anchor
the tangible experience people have each day online.
For instance, indicators like reduced exposure to
harmful content, higher satisfaction with interactions,
and diversified voices all signal a flourishing digital
community.   Monitoring these metrics creates an
empirical foundation from which platforms can evolve
responsibly.

Ethical platform design forms the backbone of such
evolution.   This involves embedding core values—

transparency, respect, and autonomy—directly into features and user interfaces. Steering away from manipulative "dark patterns" that trick users into unwanted behaviors, ethical design champions user consent by default. For example, instead of pre-checked boxes consenting to data sharing, users encounter explicit, informed choices presented in clear language. Thoughtful design also prioritizes time well spent: tools that encourage reflection before posting, or that help moderate emotionally charged conversations, nurture a kinder, more considerate atmosphere. By making ethical considerations part of the architecture, platforms honor user dignity and cultivate trust.

However, technology alone cannot carry this burden. Ownership and control matter profoundly. Distributed governance models offer promising alternatives to top-down oversight by platform owners. Consider user juries—groups of community members empowered to weigh in on contentious content or policy changes—bringing diverse perspectives to decision-making. Cooperative ownership, where users hold stakes and share in governance, transforms passive audiences into active stewards of their digital spaces. Federated moderation structures enable communities to set their own rules and enforce standards collaboratively, reflecting local values rather than imposing uniform mandates. These models share power and accountability, thereby enhancing legitimacy and community buy-in.

Interoperability and open standards are essential companions to governance innovations. When platforms operate as isolated silos, users face barriers to expression and limited freedom to migrate their social lives. Adopting open protocols and ensuring data portability dismantle such walls. Federation protocols, like those underlying decentralized networks, let users maintain identities and contacts across diverse platforms without undue control by any single provider. Enabling these cross-platform conversations reduces gatekeeping and fosters innovation by allowing smaller or niche communities to thrive alongside industry giants, thereby enriching the ecosystem's diversity.

In the shadow of dominant players, antitrust and competition policies become crucial safeguards. Without effective checks, monopolistic platforms can stifle choice and prioritize profit over public interest. Regulators worldwide are increasingly exploring measures to prevent market concentration and encourage diverse social spaces. Enforcing data-sharing mandates, scrutinizing acquisitions of potential rivals, or supporting open-source alternatives can dismantle entrenched power. A competitive social media environment fuels experimentation and responsiveness, offering users alternatives that better align with their values and needs.

Transparency in platform decision-making deepens user trust and prevents alienation. Open roadmaps reveal future feature plans and policy changes well ahead of implementation, inviting feedback and dialogue. Public feedback mechanisms—structured channels where users can propose ideas, scrutinize governance, and hold authorities accountable—democratize the platform evolution process. Governance APIs, which provide machine-readable access to moderation policies and enforcement data, enable independent researchers and civil society groups to audit platform behavior. This openness demystifies opaque algorithms and policy choices, reinforcing a healthy social contract between platforms and communities.

Yet, even a user well-versed in platform intricacies can benefit from digital literacy and education initiatives.

Empowerment through knowledge lets users navigate not only technical tools but also social dynamics and potential pitfalls. Educational programs, whether integrated into schools or offered as community workshops, teach recognition of misinformation, privacy implications, and respectful communication. Familiarity with the mechanics behind feed algorithms or data tracking arms users to make informed choices about their engagement. Thus, digital literacy acts as a vital complement to technological and governance reforms, enhancing resilience against manipulation.

Accountability mechanisms buttress these efforts by offering clear pathways to redress. Effective complaint procedures allow users to flag abuses or unfair treatment and receive timely responses. Independent oversight bodies, distanced from commercial pressures, monitor platform compliance with ethical and legal standards, increasing objectivity in evaluations. Appeals processes offer users the chance to contest decisions, ensuring fairness and avoiding arbitrary censorship. Together, these channels form a system of checks and balances essential to sustaining user trust over time.

A broader, cross-sector collaboration grounds these individual endeavors in a shared vision. Academia contributes critical research insights and ethical frameworks. Industry brings technical expertise and operational capacity. Civil society advocates for user rights and inclusivity. Their joint efforts create collective standards and best practices that extend beyond any single platform, forging a more coherent and resilient social media ecosystem. Such partnerships foster innovation while safeguarding public goods and democratizing technological progress.

Bringing these strands together suggests an actionable blueprint for healthier social media. Stakeholders—

platform developers, regulators, users, and educators
alike—must embrace well-being metrics, embed ethical
design, decentralize governance, and open systems to
interoperability. They should enact policies preserving
competition, embed transparency in decision-making,
promote widespread digital literacy, and establish
robust accountability frameworks. Through sustained
collaboration, the digital public sphere can evolve
beyond exploitative models toward spaces that uplift,
empower, and connect with integrity.

By anchoring the future of social media in these
principles and practices, we nurture an ecosystem
where technology serves human values rather than
undermines them. This is not utopian fantasy but a
principled, pragmatic pathway toward platforms that
respect complexity and foster flourishing in the digital
age.

8.7   Your Role in the Digital Society

As we navigate the vast currents of the digital realm, it
becomes clear that our participation is neither passive
nor solitary. Each individual acts as both a contributor
and a custodian of the online world, wielding influence
that ripples beyond our screens. Embracing this
responsibility begins with understanding the principles
of digital citizenship—a framework that defines our
rights alongside the duties that ensure respectful and
informed engagement.

Digital citizenship stems from the simple yet profound
notion that digital spaces mirror the complexity of
physical societies. This means that just as we expect
civility, fairness, and responsibility in face-to-face
interactions, the same values must guide our online

228

presence. Your rights include freedom of expression and privacy, but these coexist with responsibilities such as respecting others' opinions, protecting personal data, and guarding against misinformation. Recognizing this balance empowers you to cultivate an online environment where dialogue flourishes and dignity endures.

One of the most immediate expressions of responsible digital citizenship is privacy self-care. In a world where personal data is currency, managing your digital footprint has become a vital skill. Adjusting privacy settings on social media platforms, using strong and unique passwords, and remaining vigilant about the information you share are practical steps that safeguard your autonomy. Remember, every app permission granted or seemingly trivial click can build a profile that extends beyond your intentions. By actively maintaining control over your online persona, you defend not just your privacy but also your freedom from manipulation.

Critical consumption habits stand as the bulwark against the flood of information that daily demands our attention. In an era where news spreads faster than veracity can be checked, becoming a discerning consumer of digital content is a moral imperative. This involves fact-checking claims before accepting them, triangulating sources to verify reliability, and approaching sensational headlines with healthy skepticism. Mindful sharing means pausing to consider the impact of disseminating unverified information—after all, each repost or click can amplify falsehoods or deepen divisions. Cultivating such habits transforms you from a passive recipient into an active guardian of truth.

Yet, engagement online is not solely about consumption; constructive contribution is equally essential. Participating in respectful discourse requires more than avoiding harmful language—it calls for inclusive communication that appreciates diverse perspectives and acknowledges one's own biases. Using language that invites dialogue rather than confrontation sets the tone for meaningful exchanges. Being aware of unconscious biases helps prevent the amplification of stereotypes or exclusionary narratives. When your voice uplifts ideas and fosters understanding, you transform digital spaces into communities of growth and respect.

Leadership within digital communities often begins quietly but can have profound effects. Effective community leadership and moderation involve establishing clear norms, facilitating open dialogue, and resolving conflicts with fairness. Setting expectations early—whether about tone, relevance, or respect— helps create environments where everyone feels safe to contribute. When disputes arise, addressing them with empathy and firmness prevents escalation and reinforces trust. Moderators and leaders model behavior that others emulate, shaping the culture of their communities and promoting digital spaces that reflect shared values.

Beyond individual groups, advocacy and policy engagement invite you to influence the broader structures governing online life. Participating in platform governance—through feedback mechanisms, user councils, or transparency initiatives—gives voice to your concerns and helps shape features and rules that affect millions. Similarly, engaging with legislative consultations centered on digital rights and responsibilities amplifies your impact beyond the screen. Informed advocacy bridges personal experiences with systemic change, ensuring that technology evolves in ways that protect users and promote equity.

230

The digital landscape is in constant flux, making continuous learning and adaptation indispensable. Emerging risks—from new privacy threats to evolving misinformation tactics—demand ongoing vigilance. Staying informed about the latest tools, security practices, and ethical debates equips you to respond effectively to novel challenges. This might mean subscribing to reputable digital literacy resources, attending webinars, or simply being curious about new developments. Adaptation is not passive acceptance but active engagement with change, enabling you to turn challenges into opportunities for growth and resilience.

An often overlooked but invaluable contribution is peer education and mentoring. Sharing your knowledge demystifies complex topics for newcomers and strengthens collective digital competence. Whether by guiding friends through privacy settings, modeling healthy online behavior, or explaining how to spot misinformation, peer educators cultivate supportive learning environments. This ripple effect multiplies the benefits of your expertise, transforming isolated efforts into community-wide gains.

Building supportive networks reinforces these dynamics by connecting individuals around shared interests, goals, or values. Forming interest groups can provide safe spaces for discussion and collaboration, while accountability circles encourage ethical online conduct through mutual encouragement and feedback. Resource exchanges—such as sharing trusted tools or educational materials—empower members to navigate digital challenges more effectively. These networks reflect the social essence of the internet, reminding us that behind every username is a person seeking connection and understanding.

At the heart of these actions lies personal agency—the

acknowledgment that your choices, however small
they seem, collectively shape the ethical contours of
the digital society. Each decision to fact-check before
sharing, each example of thoughtful moderation, and
each act of advocacy contributes to a healthier, more
inclusive online world.   Far from being a passive
environment, the digital sphere is a shared space
constructed through countless individual acts of
participation and responsibility. Embracing your role
is both a privilege and a necessity, as together we build
the digital society we wish to inhabit.